EVERYTHING

—— but ——

TEACHING

Planning, Paperwork, and Processing

STEPHEN J. VALENTINE
Foreword by Pearl Rock Kane

CORWIN
A SAGE Company

For information:

Corwin
A SAGE Company
2455 Teller Road
Thousand Oaks, California 91320
(800) 233-9936
Fax: (800) 417-2466
www.corwinpress.com

SAGE Ltd.
1 Oliver's Yard
55 City Road
London EC1Y 1SP
United Kingdom

SAGE Pvt. Ltd.
B 1/I 1 Mohan Cooperative
   Industrial Area
Mathura Road, New Delhi 110 044
India

SAGE Asia-Pacific Pte. Ltd.
33 Pekin Street #02-01
Far East Square
Singapore 048763

Printed in the United States of America

Library of Congress Cataloging-in-Publication Data

Valentine, Stephen J.
Everything but teaching : planning, paperwork, and processing / Stephen J. Valentine; foreword by Pearl Rock Kane.
       p. cm.
Includes bibliographical references and index.
ISBN 978-1-4129-6706-8 (cloth)
ISBN 978-1-4129-6707-5 (pbk.)
    1. Teachers—Professional relationships. 2. Effective teaching. I. Title.

LB1775.2.V36 2009
371.1—dc22   2008053032

This book is printed on acid-free paper.

09   10   11   12   13   10   9   8   7   6   5   4   3   2   1

Acquisitions Editor:	Carol Chambers Collins
Editorial Assistant:	Brett Ory
Production Editor:	Veronica Stapleton
Copy Editor:	Adam Dunham
Typesetter:	C&M Digitals (P) Ltd.
Proofreader:	Dennis W. Webb
Indexer:	Kathleen Paparchontis
Cover Designer:	Michael Dubowe

Contents

Foreword

Little in my life as a student prepared me to understand the demands on a teacher. Like most people in teaching, I chose the profession because I love kids and the subjects I teach, and I want to make a difference in the world. Research studies on career decisions to enter teaching consistently show that values and idealism are what attract people to the job. They picture a life in a classroom opening minds, igniting learning, and improving the human spirit. No wonder teachers are romantics. The satisfaction of doing meaningful work and possibly changing lives forever is unparalleled.

But that is only part of the work of teaching. The real life of a teacher has another critical aspect, seldom addressed in teacher recruitment. Teaching requires strategic planning; careful record keeping; thoughtful communication; purposeful meetings with students, parents, and colleagues; and the professional responsibility to continuously learn and grow. This is the teacher's *other work*. Developing these kinds of skills requires knowledge and practice. It turns out that the skills and knowledge that got you a position as a teacher are not sufficient once in the position.

In business organizations, managers with as broad an array of task demands would be given executive coaches. The economics of schooling does not allow that to happen for teachers. That's why Stephen Valentine's book, *Everything But Teaching: Planning, Paperwork, and Processing*, is so important.

Whether you're a new teacher wondering how you can get through the day, much less the rest of the year, or a veteran teacher like myself, too often caught in predicaments that seem to occur over and over, this book can help you develop strategies and habits for a more fulfilling professional life. Valentine addresses the major demands, dilemmas, and problems of teaching and analyzes them in an informative and helpful way. Unlike most authors of teaching books, Valentine is a teacher himself. His examples of typical problems are rooted in practice and clearly recognizable. He communicates directly and personally about the everyday challenges of maintaining calendars, organizing records, providing meaningful grading and feedback, and having productive meetings.

As a skillful teacher himself, Valentine provides specific examples of what to do and what not to do. In communication with parents and students, he suggests simple guidelines for improvement. He offers sensible methods for curriculum planning. Rather than create from scratch or rehash lessons from the past, Valentine suggests archiving units. Electronic files of lesson plans, assessment samples of student work, handouts, videos, and bookmarks of related websites give busy teachers accessible and expedient choices for teaching. Being organized saves time and allows teachers to be confident in their instructional decisions. Valentine also removes guilt from those of us with unrealistic personal standards—that we never do enough—by acknowledging the gap between what is known to be the best and what is actually possible.

Most books about teaching inevitably ask teachers who are already overburdened to do more. This book asks you to think about what you value and tells you how to have a better quality work experience. It offers insight and inspiration and can help you to develop strategies and habits to increase your professional satisfaction and your value to your school. Taken seriously, this book can transform your life as a teacher.

Pearl Rock Kane
Klingenstein Family Chair Professor and Director,
The Klingenstein Center

Preface

I wrote this book for teachers, because, outside of students and my own family, I like them more than any other group of people I have ever met. I like their curiosity, their idealism, and their stubbornness. I like the wide-eyed beginners and the curmudgeonly veterans. I like them—teachers of every stripe—and I worry about them. They are too damned busy, and they are too damned conscientious. When the busyness mixes with the conscientiousness, a kind of panic ensues. We've all felt it. In teacher's lounges, on Sunday night, at six a.m., five minutes before class, or when we look across the table at our nonteaching spouses and try to explain for the millionth time that this weekend is going to be *really* busy . . . We've all felt the panic of never quite being able to catch up with our school work.

Teachers, I offer this book as a steadying force. Applied over the long haul, it will, I hope, help you catch your breath. It will help you to become more deliberate and more decisive, a steadying force for some other teacher in need of support. And it will help you make lasting contributions to your schools and the lives of your students.

I started teaching high school fresh out of a graduate program in English. Most of my pedagogical moves originated on the commonsense, gut level. I plundered my enthusiasms, planning lessons and writing tests based on what felt right. What felt right then was simple: Students would love the same books I loved; further, they would appreciate such things as the simple beauty of a Hemingway sentence, the convoluted logic of a Faulkner character, the impeccable economy of a Shakespeare couplet, the soul-stirring elegance of a Rilke sonnet. I know now that what felt right then was wrong, or at least partly wrong. These aesthetic principles were not self-evident. Enthusiasm was not enough.

I started learning this lesson—that "the gut is not enough"—early in my first year as a teacher. My department chair told me to pick a book for my second semester seniors. She didn't ask me to defend my choice; she simply told me to pick a book I liked. So I picked what, at the time, was one of my favorites, Jack Kerouac's *On the Road*. Choosing Kerouac led to one of the worst months I have ever spent in a classroom—my own, or others. It stunk, I stunk, the kids stunk. I expected the book to teach itself. The students couldn't understand why the plot seemed to repeat. I expected the narrator's romantic pilgrimages to inspire my students. They couldn't understand why the narrator kept leaving his home or why on earth he was so excited. I remember asking them over and over again, "Can't you see the beauty in this book?" and I remember them saying, over and over, "No, and we're not really interested."

Their lack of "seeing" was directly related to my fundamental grounding as a teacher. When people asked me what I taught, I listed the books and the concepts. When people asked me about my classes, I told them about the books and the concepts.

Looking back on my early years as a teacher, I notice that one mistake rises above the rest. I spent my early years in the classroom trying to convey my own personal encounters with texts. As such, I was a translator, not a teacher. I was interested in my experience, not the experience of my students. I figured that charisma and enthusiasm could pull me through. And, in all honesty, these qualities did help me. Students liked my classes, and I received great reviews from my supervisors. A few students from those days still keep in touch with me and tell me how much I helped them. After some reflection, though, I realized that any "success" gleaned from my early teaching falls into the category of luck. I made an impact on the teacher-proof kids, the ones no teacher can help or hurt very much. And the other kids, the kids who met me head on, the kids who were ridiculously advanced for their age, probably enjoyed arguing with me and probably even learned a few things. But when I think about the rest of the students in my first few classes, the great unwashed, I have no idea what I did or didn't do for them. If I did something useful, I wouldn't know it.

Now, when people ask me what I teach, I answer more simply, and I hope, more humbly: I teach kids. The change has been slow and sometimes difficult. I have been fortunate to discuss the craft of teaching with great mentors, to observe some masterful teachers, and to take part in some enlightening seminars. These experiences forced me to explore my motives for being in the classroom and to adjust some of my most deeply ingrained habits. They transformed me from a solitary reader talking *at* classes of kids to a teacher, a guide, someone as interested in how students learn as in what he can teach them.

Professional educators make deliberate choices in order to reach desired ends. Although they do not always predict every outcome or destination, they understand how to shape the journey. They can tell you, in no uncertain terms, where students started and where they ended, where they need to go and where they should be able to go. And they are effective, knowing the best way to get to the best end, even if that end is just another starting point.

In an effort to become an effective professional, I have studied best practices in the field of education, such as backward design, brain theory, and differentiated instruction. But I have also learned to embrace things that used to make my skin crawl: business models, statistics, data, and a range of analytic habits. Why? Because I realized that teaching does not begin and end in the classroom. Things that happen outside the classroom (the other work mentioned in my subtitle) can have a huge effect on what happens inside the classroom. Just ask the students of a deeply unorganized teacher how their learning is going; ask the students who are not receiving timely and thoughtful feedback on their assessments; ask the students who meet with their teachers outside of class but do not get much out of the meetings because they feel like their teacher does not really know them. Or look at your own teaching life. How many times have your best intentions for planning a great lesson been thrown off course by a frantic parent phone call or a request from an administrator? How many times have you attended a meeting without being prepared? How many times have you failed to follow up on an important student concern? As my friend and colleague Gray Smith once said, "In order to be a good teacher in today's schools, you have to be able to do *everything* well."

The bottom line is both simple and challenging: Working in the 21st-century school engages every aspect of a person's professional and personal character. To learn to cope and ultimately thrive, we need to be capable of teaching one minute, writing an incisive e-mail the next, managing a website after that, then working with a parent to develop a solution for his child, then finding ways to generate community buy-in for an important club or initiative . . . and we must learn to keep our balance while we turn from task to task.

When I was in middle and high school, I shared a love of basketball with my father. We watched a lot of games. After a few minutes of watching a game, regardless of the level of play, my father would identify the best players on the court. After a few more minutes, he would identify the single best player on the court. Then he would pose a simple and direct question: What specific actions made the best player better than the other players who were also good? During these discussions, he would not allow me to generalize. Slowly, I learned the finer points of the game and that, often, the difference between the best player and the second-best player was miniscule. The best player jumped an inch higher or a second faster. He passed to where his teammates should have been instead of where they were, leading them instead of simply responding to them. He didn't use his eyes to telegraph his passes. He had instincts to do the right things supported by skills to execute the right things effectively.

Years later, I am not surprised to find that Jim Collins (2001) has written a book called *Good to Great* wherein he systematically explores the difference between good and great companies. It seems like a natural question to ask of all enterprises worthy of attention.

In my book, I will combine my insights from watching the game of teaching with the insights I have gained from scrutinizing the thinking of other professionals who tread similar ground. My imperatives were developed from the bottom up. I did not develop a theory and then seek examples to support it. In an attempt to survive and thrive in school, I relied on ideas gleaned from teachers, educational research, management texts, and interviews with successful professionals. Along the way, I catalogued the ideas that worked, pitched the ones that did not, and then developed seven natural groupings to categorize them.

Although I have intended the book to be read in chronological order, each chapter can stand alone. In the spirit of time and busyness, you should jump around and read those chapters that match your immediate needs. With that said, each chapter title is clearly indicative of the text that will follow.

Acknowledgments

I am a fortunate man, having a network of family, friends, and colleagues who are both supportive and inspiring, who press books into my hands, who challenge me, who dare me to take on new projects, who make me laugh . . .

To Kyle Thompson, Michael Kosuda, Lisa Valentine, Justin Wiener, Laura Connolly, and Max Engel: thanks for the continuing conversations about teaching, books, work, and life.

To my colleagues at the Montclair Kimberley Academy: I cherish every day that I have the opportunity to hone my craft alongside you. Our school is a gem, and you are the light that shines through it. To Gray Smith, Dave Flocco, Denise Brown Allen, and Karen Newman: as mentors, you have taught me that a lasting and joyful career in education begins and ends with the relationships we cultivate with students and each other—it's that simple. To Mary Fitzgibbons, Tom Fox, Reverend McHugh, Andrew Von Hendy, Suzanne Matson, Stephanie Lipkowitz, and the administrative team at the Johns Hopkins Center for Talented Youth: I try to teach others the way you taught me, ever falling short.

To Carol Collins, who saw the potential in a proposal that really didn't sound like me, and asked me to write a book that did. To Brett Ory: thanks for what I know and don't know about what you did to help this book along.

To the Valentine clan: thanks for the good food, music, traditions, and unending support. To Gus and Kathi Van Eepoel, master teachers and gracious hosts: What you haven't taught me about life is probably not worth knowing. To Vicki Vega, historian, futurist, sparkplug of Sarasota: I'll keep trying to keep pace with you, but don't slow down for me.

To my colleagues at the Montclair Kimberley Academy: I cherish every day that I have the opportunity to hone my craft alongside you. Our school is a gem, and you are the light that shines through it. To Gray Smith, Dave Flocco, Denise Brown Allen, and Karen Newman: as mentors you have taught me that a lasting and joyful career in education begins and ends with the relationships we cultivate with students and each other—it's that simple.

To Mary Fitzgibbons, Tom Fox, Reverend McHugh, Andrew Von Hendy, Suzanne Matson, Stephanie Lipkowitz, and the administrative team at the Johns Hopkins Center for Talented Youth: I try to teach others the way you taught me, ever falling short. **To Peter Greer: by keeping a promise, you started teaching me about ethics from the moment I met you.**

Corwin gratefully acknowledges the contributions of the following reviewers:

Jude A. Huntz
Middle School English Teacher
The Barstow School
Kansas City, Missouri

Kate Kinnan
Sixth Grade History Teacher
Junction City Middle School
Junction City, Kansas

Loukea N. Kovanis-Wilson
Chemistry Instructor
Clarkston High School
Clarkston, Michigan

Ronald W. Poplau
Author of *The Doer of Good Becomes Good: A Primer on Volunteerism*
Kansas City, Kansas

Zsuzsanna Toth-Laughland
Mathematics Teacher
Kennett High School
Conway, New Hampshire

About the Author

Photograph by
Anthony Cuneo.

Stephen J. Valentine has worked in schools for approximately 10 years, starting in the Writing Center at the University of Virginia, then working for a summer at Exeter Academy, for several summers at The Johns Hopkins Center for Talented Youth (CTY), for two years at The Pine Crest School (Fort Lauderdale, Florida), and for the past seven years at The Montclair Kimberley Academy (Montclair, New Jersey). He has served as an academic dean (at CTY) and a teacher, advisor, department chair, and grade level chair at The Montclair Kimberley Academy; he currently serves as assistant head of the Upper School at the Montclair Kimberley Academy.

Keen on showing his literature students that he practices what he preaches, Stephen has pursued a variety of other interests in addition to his work in schools. He has been a teacher-writer for the past seven years, coauthoring a workbook about technology and publishing articles about topics ranging from teen slang to ethics. His poems have been published in *Hotel Amerika, Broken Bridge Review,* and the anthology *Red White and Blues: Poets on the Promise of America.* His first documentary film, *Somebody Loves Me: The Life and Music of Prentis Richardson,* won Best Documentary at the Nolita Film Festival in New York City and a Director's Choice award at the Park City Film Music Festival.

Stephen's educational honors include a summer Klingenstein Fellowship and a finalist award in *Education and Technology* magazine's "Ed Tech Leader of the Year" contest.

Stephen can be reached at his e-mail address, sjv@sjvalentine.com. Stephen's blog for educators can be found at www.sjvalentine.typepad.com.

Introduction

School Time
Versus Classroom Time

No matter how much you have achieved, you will always be merely good relative to what you can become. Greatness is an inherently dynamic process, not an end point. The moment you think of yourself as great, your slide toward mediocrity will have already begun.

—Jim Collins, *Good to Great and the Social Sectors*

I have seen a lot of good teachers exist on the brink of failure. These educators know their content, have a passion for their subject, and get along with kids. So, what's the problem?

The problem is something I call the *25-percent piranha*. Ideally, educators should spend most of their time, let's say 75 percent, teaching, planning to teach, grading assessments, or meeting with individual students. This classroom time, to me, is the essential part of teachers' jobs. They should spend the rest of their time, their school time, performing other duties. These other duties could be coaching, talking with parents, attending faculty meetings, or writing reports. In my experience, though, the other 25 percent has a funny habit of tearing off chunks of time from the essential 75 percent. For a variety of reasons—some of which are created by administrators or unspoken public relations pressures, some of which are created by poor habits—teachers either consciously or unconsciously give their peak energy and attention to things that happen outside the classroom. As a result, they often enter their classrooms with less deliberate intentions than they should, they return papers much later than they should, they "grab an old lesson that worked" instead of differentiating for their current batch of students, or they simply wear themselves into the ground by trying to do everything.

Schools have become increasingly complex work environments, and the job of teaching is becoming increasingly fragmented. Teachers constantly pass my office at school and say things like, "I wish I could just teach," or, "It seems like I haven't had time to grade in weeks." In my own complicated job, I often feel like I have to fight my way out of meetings, off the phone, or away from e-mails just to get to my classroom on time. Frankly, I enjoy the challenge, and I do believe that we can accomplish a great deal during our school time. But in order to be successful, I have had to learn to be effective. In this book, I will attempt to share what I've learned and to model the attitude that has allowed me to continue to learn in our rapidly changing schools.

To be clear, this book is not about making people better teachers *in* the classroom. It is not about differentiated instruction or backward design or how to organize a class period. Instead, it is about the other skill set (the survival skill set) that people need in order to stay afloat at school, and it is motivated by the idea that we can enrich student learning by effectively handling outside-the-classroom responsibilities and priorities.

When I work with teachers who are having trouble in the classroom, I usually try to dig around the edges to see how they are spending their free periods. Are they planning enough or are they bogged down with administrative details? Are they dealing effectively with their e-mails or are they simply letting their inboxes fill up with unanswered posts, causing endless anxiety about what's not getting done? Are they keeping track of what they learn during student conferences or while grading student assessments, and then using this knowledge to clarify or redirect their future work with students? By exploring these blurred edges, these hidden nooks of teachers' lives, I hope to aid teachers in bringing their peak talents and energies to their teaching, thereby taming the 25-percent piranha.

THE CHALLENGE OF WORKING IN OUR SCHOOLS

At times, the very things that make people talented educators (passion, single-minded dedication to the craft, a storehouse of knowledge that can only be used in a particular discipline) cause them to struggle in school environments. These talented teachers are sometimes the same people who are perpetually late to meetings (or miss them altogether), who miss deadlines, who are unprepared for meetings with parents, or who have trouble with public speaking. In short, they have trouble tending to the other 25 percent of their job. Give them a Robert Frost poem or a challenging physics problem and a class of kids, and they are dazzling; ask them to wow a classroom of parents at back-to-school night and you have a dozen parents asking to have their kids removed from the class. Bottom line: some teachers struggle at school whenever they are not in their classrooms. In a perfect world, this struggle would not matter. But in the real world of education, it creates two problems. First, it creates a problem for the school that constantly has to vouch for such teachers. Second, and more important, this struggle wears away at teachers' psyches. They know they are falling short, and either they don't care (which is highly unprofessional), or their shortcomings lead them to negative feelings about themselves or about their schools. Neither scenario is a good one for students in the long run.

The following vignettes illustrate this current reality.

Vignette 1

Young, Eager, and Discouraged

Recently, I sat down with one of the most talented young teachers I know. She has an excellent education and a quick mind, and she loves her students and her subject. I'll call her Jill. It was early August, and we had completed a rigorous day at a conference on assessment. During our final breakout session, as I eagerly listed all the innovations I planned to make in my classroom, Jill looked increasingly uncomfortable. When she finally spoke, she said, "Steve, I'm just not as excited as you are about all of this. You seem to understand exactly where all these changes will fit into your plans, but I'm going to start September with a list of dozens of things I would like to try. Of course, I want to use more formative assessment. And of course I want to vary my teaching practices. When I hear these ideas, I know they are important. But if I'm being honest with myself, I know I'll probably go back to teaching exactly like I did last year. I hardly slept last year. I could barely keep up. Even if I want to change, I'm not sure that I can."

This young teacher's genuine reaction reminded me of my early years as a teacher. I remembered attending a lecture at the Klingenstein Summer Institute and hearing a headmaster from a very successful school lecture about Fenstermacher and Soltis's three stances of teaching. He discussed liberationist-style teachers, therapist-style teachers, and executive-style teachers. The Teacher's College Press (2000) website lists the following brief summaries of each stance:

- The *Executive* approach views the teacher as a skillful manager of learning and the acquisition of knowledge, skills, understandings, and competencies.
- The *Facilitator* approach (previously called the therapist approach) has been renamed and reconceived to allow for a more global consideration of teachers who focus on the development and nurturing of each student's unique capacities and personal characteristics to attain authenticity and self-actualization.
- The *Liberationist* approach views the teacher as a liberator of the mind. The classical liberationist stresses initiation into ways of knowing and the development of the student's intellectual and moral virtues. (para. 3–5)

This headmaster wanted to work with teachers who were liberationists, but he said that he would greatly prefer that teachers started off as executives in, and out of, the classroom.

When I heard that lecture, I was just like Jill—eagerly starting my career—and I didn't agree with the headmaster's comments. Teaching, for me, was an opportunity to change the way students saw the world. I wanted them to see the world the way writers did. I wanted them to challenge every system of thought, every conclusion, every rule. I entered teaching to be a liberationist, and when I heard the definition of that term I immediately identified with it.

The flaw in my design was that, like Jill, I became so busy at school that I did not have the time to develop appropriate scaffolds to lead students into the kind of thinking (and liberation) for which I hoped. I became frustrated when students didn't "get it," and I naturally taught toward the students who were gifted enough to attain liberation on their own, with or without teachers.

These days, I am still interested in the liberationist stance in teaching, and I strive for it. But I am much more respectful of the executive stance, and I have employed it frequently to ensure that students reach the intellectual "promised land." This requires more attention to rubrics, more formative assessments designed to check for understanding, and more attention paid to students who miss class and need gaps filled.

If my executive skill inside and outside the classroom has compounded my ability to be the kind of teacher I want to be, it has also modified my expectations for potential colleagues. Throughout my career, I have frequently screened job candidates. When hiring teachers, I want to find people who have a passion for their subject. I want fire and intuition.

And of course, I want people who understand kids, curriculum, how to run a classroom, and how to teach. But in the increasingly complex world of schools, I also have to find ways to assess organizational ability; I have to assess candidates' writing to make sure they can communicate in a clear and professional manner; I have to ask about their ability to meet deadlines. Increasingly, the bottom line for schools is that effective teachers survive and thrive while less-effective teachers, or teachers who are downright unorganized and unfocused, have a difficult time.

For the less-effective educators, school is not a joy, and it is often joyless to work with them. Often, they resist bureaucracy (which is occasionally a good thing), and they often resist change (which is rarely a good thing). Their resistance, I believe, can be directly tied to the fact that they have trouble juggling their teaching load with things that take place outside the classroom.

Fortunately, Jill has the kinds of skills that will allow her to beat back the world and focus on her teaching. At our breakout session, I encouraged her to rely on her organizational skills and her time-management skills. Those things would make her second year more relaxed. No one expected her to improve 38 ways each year. But if she approached improvement in a disciplined way, picking three or four things to work on, setting up checkpoints and measures to gauge their success, she would quickly know, at year's end, which practices to keep and which practices to dump in favor of something new.

Vignette 2

Old Timers and Professional Development

It's the Tuesday before Thanksgiving at a school in New England. For this particular school, a long professional development (PD) day looms before a much needed three-day break. A group of veterans who call themselves "The Old Timers" sit in the back of the lecture hall. They've seen the trends come and go and come again. They're each about three to five years from retirement, but they are still sharp. They get good results in the classroom, and the community depends on them for their historical perspective, their wisdom, and their well-tempered cynicism.

The old timers will go through this PD day in the same way they have gone though all the others—with good-humored barbs and occasionally vigorous participation. Although they are outwardly against PD days, this is just an act they put on for the benefit of their little group. They actually enjoy a good lecture followed by some breakout sessions. Privately, they will tell you that some of the speakers they have seen over the years have been "clever," and that they "generally have something to offer." But for them, professional development is somewhat like a video game—a compelling distraction. It might mimic real teaching, but it won't make anyone better at real teaching.

What is needed for growth, for sheer progress in the 21st-century school, is the time and organization skills necessary to meet the demands of change. Although I do not know for sure, I would be willing to bet that most schools would rather invest in a speaker to present on a recent educational innovation or insight rather than an organization and time-management specialist. Is it any wonder that many teachers like the old timers discussed above are resistant to change? True change requires a complete restructuring of their way of doing business, the way that has served them well for decades. The overall goal of professional development may be the same—to serve students and their learning needs—but the time needed to change is simply not available.

WHAT GIVES?

Each of the vignettes above has a similar theme: smart, competent teachers cannot or will not improve or advance if they do not address certain conditions of their work environment. Jill needed to learn how to negotiate the demands of her community. The old timers had to determine to change their ingrained work habits to make time and space for improvement.

Although these examples focus on things that happen outside the classroom, what's really at stake is the classroom itself. The stream of work that flows into the classroom (from teacher to student) and out of the classroom (from student to teacher) needs to be protected, not littered. If teachers cannot process the out-of-class demands placed on their time, they will bring less to the classroom and respond to students with less agility and less focus.

Unfortunately, there is no easy way to keep the streams pure, clear, and clean. Even good teachers with superior organization skills and an unflagging commitment to innovation can get bogged down with responsibilities that have only a tangential relationship to the teaching they do in the classroom. Take, for example, my friend and former colleague, Dr. Denise Brown Allen. Once, in an exasperated state, she signed an e-mail (personal communication, March 2008) with a list of roles that she plays. A clever satire of the typical executive signature, her list included: Club Advisor, Supervisor, Advisor, Teacher, Curriculum Designer, Action Planner, Parent, Arbitrator, Planner, Recruiter, Admissions Committee

Member, Negotiator, Department Chair, Spouse, Event Planner, Neighbor, Colleague, Student, Coach, Therapist, Confidante, Accountant, Chauffer, Travel Agent, and Chaperone. One of the most talented, hardworking people I know, Dr. Brown Allen was clearly bumping up against the overwhelming demands of a frenzied workplace. Although she was poking fun at the situation, the situation was clearly dire.

Let's look a bit more closely. During one of the busiest times of my recent school year, I decided to log my daily professional activities. I was following the advice set forth in the Donald Graves (2001) book, *The Energy to Teach*. He encourages teachers to keep a log and then analyze that log. This is a solid practice for any professional, and I have seen it championed in several business texts including Peter Drucker and J. A. Marciarello's (2006) excellent guidebook about effectiveness, *The Effective Executive in Action: A Journal for Getting the Right Things Done*.

I kept a log for only four days. In my log, after the last entry, I simply wrote, "I'm much too busy and tired to continue keeping a log." This was after only two days at work. My log reads as follows:

Saturday

- Leave the house at 11
- Arrive at school for homecoming at 12. As 12th-grade dean, I have to supervise the senior barbecue.
- Work with 12th-grade class to sell food
- Leave at 4:00

Sunday

- Write comments for midsemester. Each comment is roughly a half page. Although I only teach 50 students, this takes me much of the day. I have little to no time for preparation or grading.

Monday

- I spend the day in a conference room grading practice SAT-style essays for students in Grades 10 and 11. This runs from 8–3. A sub teaches my students.
- I finish my comments for midsemester, left over from the night before (5–7)
- Work on college recommendations (9–11)

Tuesday

- 7–8 meeting
- I teach for approximately three hours on Tuesday.

- During my downtime, I proofread comments for colleagues (part of my job as department chair) and work on college recommendations.
- I attend another meeting after school for one hour.
- When I arrive at home, I proofread more comments for two hours.

Traditionally, time-management texts would encourage a person to eliminate actions without significant payoff or without a clear connection to one's job. But virtually everything on my list has a significant payoff for students and a clear connection to my job. Research shows that it is beneficial for students to interact with teachers outside the classroom, and so my trip to homecoming was important. Well-written reports that are sent home to parents are important, and a teacher should spend as much time as necessary making sure these reports are detailed and useful. Clearly, college recommendations are important. And clearly, giving the student body an accurate projection of their standardized test scores is important. So, what gives? What *can* give?

TIME, HABITS, AND A COMMITMENT TO CONTINUAL IMPROVEMENT

Teaching is a privileged position in that teachers have an opportunity to work with children, our best national resource, in a position outside the corporate world where employees often have to bill their hours and track their financial profits. But teaching is not so privileged that it can ignore the insights of other professions. Teachers spend a large chunk of their time at school in places other than the classroom. How they spend that time has a huge impact on the caliber of their professional affiliation with students, parents, and schools.

A quick glance at my own teaching schedule (from last year) shows that I spent roughly 13 hours a week in class and roughly 27 hours a week outside of class (a blessed schedule, I know). On my best days, I used my nonteaching time productively. I corresponded with parents, met with students, researched, planned lessons, and graded. I delivered speeches to the student body; negotiated with administrators, parents, and students; and made good decisions. All these actions made me a better educator; all these actions informed my practice in the classroom. I don't have to tell you that there were also days when I was less effective outside the classroom, days when I did not approach tasks with clarity, days when I simply was overwhelmed.

While this book will examine parts of classroom life, it will mostly concern itself with what happens outside the classroom in preparation for, and in order to augment, student learning. In modeling a commitment to finding what works for teaching professionals, I will

1. Break down the common elements of the job of teachers, looking particularly at those seven elements that compose the time when teachers are not in the classroom

2. Apply best practices from other professions and within the profession to help teachers vastly improve their approach to these common elements

3. Provide teachers with a range of resources to have a positive and direct influence on their professional growth and effectiveness

A commitment to continual improvement, to getting the right things done in schools, requires that we look *at ourselves and outside ourselves.* The rest of this book not only will be packed with useful tips and strategies but also will push educators to engage in the kind of organization and reflection that is necessary for constant improvement. I will focus on several habits of mind that I believe give teachers the most leverage.

First, I will present the concepts of forward thinking and effective planning. Many problems and organizational snafus can be avoided, saving time for the important work of teaching. Second, I will introduce and elaborate on the analytic approach to problem solving as it relates to student learning. Much literature has called for leaders who function as problem solvers (see, in particular, Schmoker, 1999). I will translate this idea into a workable form for educators, giving them the tools to solve their own problems in ways that (1) cause the problem to stay solved and (2) inform future practice. Finally, I will present insights regarding the deliberate and careful organization of time, materials, and student data. By developing the proper habits outside the classroom, a teacher can generate continual grist for the analytic mill, fueling ongoing learning and student improvement.

Imperative 1

Plan Your Time Wisely

Aside from their lesson plans, many teachers have a vague sense of what they want to accomplish on any given day; consequently, when the school day starts, they are simply washed through the hallways and spit out at the end of the last period. Certainly, they can have a meaningful impact on students; certainly, they can be productive educators. But most of them are not using time as effectively as they might. I want to change the way teachers relate to time. I want them to think about time the way conductors think about sound. Each day can be a symphony rather than a muddled mess that ends with a dry throat, an exhausted thump in any chair that will have you, and a vague sense of unease about things left undone and problems left unsolved. The idea is to make things happen, and not just allow things to happen to you.

Successful educators are mindful and intentional. They constantly ask themselves why they are presenting certain lessons, how they are dealing (or not dealing) with certain students, and what they might be doing next week or the week after to create continuity in their classes. Planning one's outside-the-classroom time can eliminate undue anxiety and, therefore, help sharpen teachers' minds when they enter their classrooms. I tell teachers that anytime they have their plan book open, they are being productive and improving their effectiveness. Personally, I devote some time each week to sitting in a quiet place and reviewing my commitments for the week, my deadlines, and my expected outcomes.

I encourage you to view time as something that you generate, not something that preys on you. And your new relationship with time begins with your calendar.

YOUR CALENDAR

Spending time thinking about calendars might be the last thing in the world you'd expect passionate teachers would do. Rather, you might expect that they would commit their time to addressing curriculum, teaching strategies, and kids, right? Of course. But passionate commitment is best supported by clear systems for managing the daily influx of appointments and information that crowd our minds and lives. Without a strong, functional way to keep track of actions, events, appointments, and deadlines, you will be scattered—too scattered to give your full self to the task of education. Just as your body's functionality, its strength and balance, radiates from your core, your calendar must be strong if you hope to function with agility, quickness, precision, and some semblance of control in a school community.

We all keep calendars, but most of us can tighten up our calendaring skills. To that end, a good practice is to acknowledge that the calendar should be a sacred space for responsibilities that absolutely *must get done* and are absolutely tied to *specific dates and times* (Allen, 2001, pp. 39, 41). Although the point might seem like common sense, teachers need to be reminded (or trained) to have one place and one place only where they write down their appointments. Too many teachers use messy sticky notes or scraps of paper to keep track of important commitments.

When teachers mismanage their calendars, they become forgetful (or only remember the big assembly, for instance, when they see someone else going to it). They miss or are tardy to meetings; they are unprepared for classes or other commitments; they fail to return phone calls or e-mails in a timely fashion; they miss deadlines. The effects of a mismanaged calendar undermine the foundation of a school thereby eroding positive thoughts and feelings about the school. Every school employee is the caretaker of the school's mission and meaning. Botched appointments unnerve those who are prepared, those who are expecting input or a response from you, and all those who rely on your professionalism. On the other hand, if you establish a dynamic calendar, as I outline below, then you will have a strong core, and your commitment to the task of education will be supported.

Choosing a Calendar

To establish a dynamic calendar you must first choose a calendar, one calendar that will hold all your appointments. There are many types of calendars, including large, desk calendars, pocket calendars, notebook-style calendars, and electronic calendars on your computer or handheld device. Choose a calendar that you understand, one that is portable, and one that can be updated or modified quickly and efficiently. Also, choose a calendar that has relatively short time demarcations.

YOUR DYNAMIC CALENDAR

Calendar choice aside, what I'm interested in here is spurring you to think more actively about your calendar. Once you get the hang of listing all your commitments in one place at the precise time you need to do them (as recommended by Allen, 2001), you are ready to start using your calendar in a more dynamic way—to meet the needs of your community and your own, personal educational mission.

Technophobes take heart. Using your calendar in a more dynamic way does not require you to synch a handheld device with a computer, upload data to a web-based program, or transfer deadlines from one iCalendar to another. While these options can be useful to someone who is familiar with the technologies, dynamic calendaring is more along the lines of a skill set that you can use and transfer to any type of calendar. You must decide what works for your situation. If the latest technological gadgets work for you, charge them and get ready to use them. If not, sharpen your pencils. Either way, your first task is to gather and list your responsibilities so they are set clearly before you each day.

Responsibilities—Planning to Do What You Must Do

If your school has a good master calendar, this task should take about an hour, and it will save you many hours of disruption. If your school does not have a good master calendar, then work with what you have and take the time to supplement your calendar with what you can. The time spent at the front end will pay off immeasurably.

To build your own calendar, one that will ensure certainty, first you need to find your school's master calendar or any calendar on which your responsibilities appear, and make a copy of it. Save the original in a file. Read through the extra copy for anything you absolutely must do, and circle those items. You are looking for things like grading deadlines, parent conference days, inservice, any meetings for which your presence is required, and special schedules. Circle these responsibilities. Then, as you read through the master calendar a second time and copy the circled items into your personal calendar system, put an X through each circle. Make sure that you account for start times and end times. You should not simply list items in your calendar; block out the time required. Next, read through the calendar a third time, looking only at the items that are not crossed out. Finally, you are ready to add your class schedule to your calendar. Again, walk through each week, adding both the classes and their block of time.

It pays to be thorough in this task. Once you have completed it, you will derive a sense of confidence from the fact that you know where you must be and when you must be there. Also, and perhaps more important, you have identified all the blank spaces in your calendar. Blank calendar space and how you use it is the true test of a complete teacher, one who will make contributions both inside and outside the classroom.

Priorities—Planning to Do What You Value

The two educators I remember best from high school are Tom Fox, my basketball coach, and Mary Fitzgibbons, my English teacher. Aside from some memories from the court and the classroom, what I remember best about these two are things that happened outside their usual domains of influence. Coach Fox used to show up at my other sporting events; for example, I remember, clear as day, an important track meet. Coach Fox showed up for my event, the two-mile run, perhaps the most boring and longest event at a track meet, and talked me through each lap each time I passed him in the stands. Mrs. Fitzgibbons, too, went above and beyond the call of duty by helping me arrange a writing portfolio for a creative writing conference. This had nothing to do with grammar or critical writing or the other things that went on in her classroom.

When I think about these educators, I realize that these extra, unpaid activities reflected completely their values as educators. Coach Fox believed in student athletes; he believed in supporting them in all their athletic endeavors; he believed in supporting other coaches and teams as well, serving as a fine model for collegiality. And Mrs. Fitzgibbons believed in creativity and poetry even though she had to spend most of her time in the classroom teaching students about the fundamentals of sentence construction or how to understand the surface meaning of Shakespeare's sonnets. The "extra" things these adults did for me to support my growth still stick with me 15 years later. Coach Fox and Mrs. Fitzgibbons transcended the data about "what works" and the trends in educational pedagogy by simply following their own educational passions and understanding how to articulate and live their educational missions.

Therefore, I offer a challenge: Once you have filled in your responsibilities, your "must dos," look at the white space as if you are an artist looking at a blank canvas. This is where you can sketch your personal vision of education, of what matters to you in school communities.

William James said that "our beliefs and our attention are the same fact" (Richardson, 2006, pp. xxiii–xiv). Do you want to support the arts in your school? Contact your school's art teachers, band leaders, or drama coaches. Ask them to see the schedule of student events, and put a few of them on your calendar. Do you want to tutor students who perpetually underachieve? Talk to the person in your school responsible for collecting data such as student grades and PSAT scores. Identify the students who really need help, then carve out the time for them. Do you want to write an educational article for a journal? Lead a community service initiative? Help students with study skills? Plan for these endeavors, in writing, on your calendar.

If you are having trouble identifying your educational mission and values, you owe it to yourself, your school, and your students to take a few minutes to think about your personal motivation for working in schools.

Personal Alignment

When I first started writing, over a decade ago, a fortuitous experience with Vin Scelsa's radio program, *Idiot's Delight*, led me to a copy of Rainer Marie Rilke's *Letters to a Young Poet*. I remember being deeply moved by the opening letter wherein Rilke challenges his young apprentice to consider the root causes of his vocation. He poses a difficult question: *Must you write?*

The answer, I think, is less important than the asking. As in most of Rilke's work, he is not simply trying to provoke a simple yes or no. He wants his apprentice to locate and tap a hidden source of energy, one that emerges from inside the young writer.

So I ask you, *must you teach?* What draws you to this curious occupation that promises neither fame nor fortune? What draws you to this work that cuts into nights and weekends, that never feels finished or final?

Some of the root causes for why people teach I have heard about over the years include a love of kids, subject, learning, variety, people, and human nature; an aversion to corporations; and a belief that we can change the world one young person at a time.

Imagine a school where people were driven by such causes instead of the usual drivers (i.e., speed, parents, test scores, administration). Getting back to Rilke, then, I would ask, How can we move from these internal motives, these secret springs of energy, to focused, efficient, sustainable systems in our day-to-day teaching life? How can we realign our daily habits and practices with our innermost convictions and beliefs about education? The questions in Figure 1.1 can help.

Figure 1.1

Clarifying Your Personal Mission

At the end of your career, for what do you want to be remembered? (Think in terms of students, colleagues, and parents.)

_____

_____

_____

What do you value in your personal life? Can you apply your personal values to your work as an educator?

_____

_____

_____

Why do you work in a school? What drew you to this kind of work, and what keeps you going?

_____

_____

_____

Value-Added Checklist—Based on your answers above, generate a list of 5 to 10 items that articulate your values in terms of specific, school-related activities. Use the following formulas to generate your list:

I value _____ ; therefore, in school, I will _____

_____

_____

_____

OR

I believe that _____ ; therefore, in school, I will _____

_____

_____

_____

Although this kind of activity may seem useless to some of the more practical-minded or seasoned teachers, I contend that this process is one of the most practical forms of thinking in which a teacher, or any busy professional, can engage. We build up so much professional flab that it's hard to see the teachers underneath sometimes. The process I'm recommending helps you to be clear (first with yourself, then with others) about how to spend your discretionary time (the time not explicitly concerned with your direct responsibilities). For example:

- If you have determined that you value and want to model a "greener" approach to school life, you can focus on finding ways to send most documents via e-mail or to post them on a website, and encourage this practice in others.
- If you have determined that you value one-on-one interactions with students, you can block out some time after school to meet with students. You can write this into your curriculum plan (assigning times when each student must meet with you), and your calendar will slowly conform to your aspirations. Ideally, if this kind of interaction is gratifying to you, you will also start to feel even better about the work you do.
- If you value the idea of being a teacher and a coach, perhaps you can find a way to do even more coaching.

If you know what you value and you are clear about it, you can slice right through the fog and noise of a school day and begin to build the kind of school life that will tap into your particular strengths and your most personal source of energy. This is how to find your voice as an educator.

Activating Priorities

An interesting way to think about your priorities, once you have isolated them, is to imagine yourself as the leader in a new, small business venture within the larger "corporation" of your school. Guy Kawasaki (2004), who directs a venture capital firm and helped develop the Macintosh computer, refers to this in a corporate environment as *internal entrepreneuring*. Although meant for corporate-type employees who aspire to create innovative products and services within their companies, Kawasaki's advice regarding internal entrepreneuring also applies to teachers who aspire to start new clubs or initiatives in their current schools. Helpful "Kawasakaisms" (pp. 19–23) to keep in mind are adapted for educators below.

- Your innovation should be aimed, first and foremost, at improving the school and the lives of students.
- If possible, build on an existing program or trend.
- Galvanize other teachers; their support will be crucial, especially if your innovation becomes a schoolwide initiative.
- Collect data and share it. Schools are dynamic places, and teachers can always use data to inform their decisions.

Forecasting/Problem Solving

Once you have established (and calendared) your responsibilities and your priorities, you can use your calendar on a weekly or monthly basis to spot those black holes of time that can dismantle a day or a week.

For example, if you have a due date for college recommendations and you expect that you will be writing some, you can go through and block out some time around the deadline. If you know that a particular cumulative assessment (like exams) or a particular recommendation (like honors or AP) is likely to generate a few hours of parent phone calls or meetings, block out some time around those events. Certain stretches of the school year become ridiculously stressful because we are trying to do our daily jobs, our extra jobs, our hoped for jobs, our put off jobs . . . and then a big, unexpected event comes along and throws off the fragile balance. You can expect and plan for the unexpected by being realistic about the potentially percussive moments in your schedule. After a few years of really paying attention to the job, you should be able to predict the unexpected and block out time for it.

For now, then, allow your mind to range through the year by flipping through your emerging calendar. What could go wrong? How can you avoid it? What could go right? How can you make sure it happens? What do you want to measure? Automate? Study the trends in your own past calendars. What things get you, year after year? When do you run out of gas? If you simply don't know the answer to these questions, you have to do a better job of reflecting.

Reflecting

As you move through your calendar during the school year, and close out your weeks, find a place on the calendar (in a corner or an unused section of a paper calendar, or on an electronic calendar, like iCalendar, as an attachment) where you can take notes on the way things are unfolding for you. The purpose of this kind of activity is to create a resource (from your own hard work) that you can use in the future to plan more effectively.

The following kinds of notations are short and efficient and will give you plenty of information when you need it. In fact, you can even copy them into the front of your calendar and simply use their numbers as a shorthand reflection.

1. This activity took much longer than expected.

2. This activity took a lot less time than expected.

3. This activity was a complete waste of time and should be discussed with an administrator.

4. This activity was poorly run.

5. I would like to do more of this next year.

6. I would like to do less of this next year.

7. This activity was highly stressful for me (unexpected).

8. This activity was highly stressful for me (expected).

9. This activity, when repeated next year, will require a great deal of planning.

10. This activity needs to be systematized.

11. This activity left me feeling energized and positive.

12. This activity left me feeling drained and negative.

13. This activity was easy to do.

Downtime/Recovery

The Winter 2007 issue of the *Harvard Business Review* is devoted to stamina, mental agility, and resilience, among other things. One article (Chapman, 2007), "Are You Working Too Hard? A Conversation With Mind/Body Researcher Herbert Benson," champions the "breakout principle," wherein workers access insights and creativity by alternately working on problems and then walking away from them for a short period of time.

Teachers hate to stop working. They often feel too guilty or overwhelmed to take a break. Although breaking away from one's job tasks might seem counterintuitive if you actually want to complete those tasks, examples of the benefits of rest, rejuvenation, occasional changes of pace or perspective, and reflection are legion.

- Frank Boyden, the famous Headmaster at Deerfield, used to take short naps in his office during the day (McPhee, 1992).
- The 20 percent rule at Google states that "software engineers spend at least 20 percent of their time, or one day a week, working on whatever project [interests] them." This rule is designed to spur bottom-up innovation by allowing employees to explore their passions (Vise & Malseed, 2006, pp. 131–132).
- Charles Munger, Warren Buffet's number two man, in an interview in *Kiplinger's* (Goldberg, 2005, para. 6), mentioned that, "Warren and I do more reading and thinking and less doing than most people in business." They allow themselves space and time to figure out their next big moves.

Teachers must be willing to take a step back from the daily grind. This takes a bit of courage, a bit of planning, a bit of toughness. But long-term performance hangs in the balance. Burnout doesn't help anyone. Tired thinking or grading or planning lacks the essential crispness that attracts the quick minds of the young. Effective teachers would be wise to plan time for relaxation, time to let the mind wander, time to fully recover from the demands of school life, time to think about long-term goals and ambitions . . . and to ink these "rejuvenation events" into their calendars.

Nets

All this talk about rejuvenation reminds me of a story. Once, when I was a teenager, I went fishing with my father and the best fisherman he knew. I remember rolling up to the lake, much too early for my taste, and unpacking my badly packed gear. Then I remember looking in my tackle box, which had not been cleaned or organized in a while. Rusted, musty hooks and gear were twisted in frazzled line and wire. By the time I made it to the water (just a minute or so behind my father, I might add) his friend, the great fisherman, had already hauled a fish right into his battered but reliable fishing net. My father turned to me and said, "The best fishermen always get their lines in the water first. You'll see that again and again."

Years later, I continue to agree with that statement (although I wouldn't have admitted this when I was a teenager), and it has continued to prove relevant. The best fishermen understand that time "on the lake" is sacred and that they probably have left other commitments to carve out such time. This gives their action clarity and focus, a leanness and simplicity that knows exactly what it seeks. They don't suffer fools gladly, as the saying goes. They know exactly what they hope to catch, and they always are ready for the special, surprise fish, the extraordinary event, for which they have sharpened their skills over the years.

Much like fishermen, when teachers approach school, we need to know what we are trying to catch. We need to know what kind of bait to use to catch certain fish. We need to be sure our poles are in good shape, our tackle is organized and clean. We need to be ready for the miraculous appearance of what filmmaker David Lynch (2006), to twist the analogy a little bit further, calls the "really big fish." And we need to have our nets ready to scoop up the catch, whatever it is.

So, part of planning involves thinking about what you want to catch (students doing). You can worry later about measuring the fish and weighing them and maybe photographing them for posterity or evidence. But first you must plan your catch. Do you want to catch data that show where students begin and where they end with a certain skill set? Do you want to catch an entire class's score on a grammar test in order to give the previous year's teachers a snapshot of what students retained? Do you want to catch the number of detentions students receive for a particular kind of offense that relates to a specific kind of school climate issue (say, respect) that you want to improve? Do you want to catch the best student work you see?

The other part of planning involves having your nets ready to scoop up the catch. Here are some simple nets I have set up in the past. I fill them in as I go, without thinking about the content.

- An Excel spreadsheet with established categories to measure student progress on writing assessments.
- A link to an intranet website for displaying exceptional student work as it comes in. I set up the template for this site in advance, so I can simply and easily upload the student work with the help of a basic scanner. (This has the secondary consequence of motivating students to write papers that are good enough to appear on the site.)
- A manila folder for notes and e-mails (printed out) relevant to a faculty newsletter I write each spring.

I examine these nets when they are full to (1) answer questions I might have about curriculum or students, (2) contribute to future lesson plans or learning opportunities, or (3) complete my future work in a more timely and thorough fashion.

NOW YOU CAN RELAX

One of the best moments of my workweek occurs on Sunday night, after I put my son to bed. I set aside about an hour to think through my week, adding to my calendar things that I want to happen, winding my clock. I think about my priorities to make sure that my week will accomplish not only what I need to (what is dictated), but also what I truly value. When this work is done, I relax. I know the week can now become intuitive. I know where I will dock my ship, when I will go out to sea, when I will start and stop, when I will need to perform, and what I need to accomplish. The rest will be a surprise, one that will ask me to use any talent, will, luck, and charm I can muster, one that will make me laugh or gasp at the staggering range of humanity on display in our schools. Because my responsibilities are clearly noted, and my priorities clearly articulated, I know I will be fully open to participation in the reality of school life. This chapter and this book are not about becoming robotic in your pursuits: They intend to free you to do the kind of work of which you are capable and that only you can do.

Imperative 2

Tailor Your Grading and Feedback to Suit the Needs of Your Students

Most of the teachers I know are grading as fast as they can, trying to make up for being behind by moving at such blazing speeds that they hand off graded work to students as if it is a hot potato. Teachers are doing their best. Simultaneously, debates rage on among teacher-writers, researchers, and academics. Should we even give grades? How can we use feedback to transform learning communities? What kind of feedback is most effective?

Anyone who has ever worked in professional development knows the difficulty of closing the gap between what is *known to be best* and what is *actually possible,* in practice, for busy teachers. As we think through and begin to apply assessment strategies, here's what must not happen: The perfect must not become the enemy of the good. Most schools cannot adopt full-scale programs dictated by the experts. Most schools cannot eliminate the standard grading system or the "importance" of standardized tests (not anytime soon, that is). Regardless, most schools can encourage educators to adopt some of the strategies suggested by current research on assessment. Every teacher provides feedback (of some sort) on assessments, and most teachers calculate grades.

Here, then, is what must happen: To move forward as teachers, regardless of our comfort level with assessment theory, we need to identify where the research fits most naturally into daily practice. We need to think about and modify how we prepare students and ourselves for assessment, and what we do with assessments after they are complete. The idea is to approach our time with students with as much clarity as possible and to maximize the time we already spend on the grading process, one of our most important tasks.

THREE CAUTIONARY TALES

In this chapter, I examine three vignettes from my own history as an assessor. These stories are designed to show you how assessment insight arises naturally from a reflective practice and a close engagement with students; at the same time, they will show you where robust assessment strategies might fit most naturally, and least invasively, in a busy school environment.

Vignette 1

The worst advice I ever received about assessment and feedback was, sadly, the first advice I ever received about assessment and feedback. As I shuffled off to my first class of the year, the first class of my career, an old guard faculty member pulled me aside and said, "All I'll tell you is that when you turn back a paper or a test, hold on to that sucker until the last possible moment . . . until the kids are about ready to bust through the door. This will all but guarantee that you won't hear any complaints. By the time any of your students think about challenging a grade, they will be caught up in something else. You know how kids are." Even as an amateur on my first day on the job, I knew that I was unequivocally hearing what Harry Gordon Frankfurt (2005), professor emeritus of philosophy at Princeton University, would call "bullshit."

Insight # 1

We must not be afraid of feedback or grades or the response they might generate from students or parents. Providing clear and direct feedback is what we do. It's at the heart of our profession.

According to Pollock (2007) and Stiggins (2007), feedback should be focused on learning or achievement targets (p. 105, pp. 63–35). Davies (2007) adds that feedback should be specific and descriptive: "Less effective feedback merely judges the learning (for example, 'Good job!' or 'Needs work!'), while specific, descriptive feedback related to criteria informs learners about what they have done well and what they need to do differently" (p. 32). Taken in this light, feedback becomes simple and uncontroversial, unclouded by emotion or the burden of judgment. I believe it is crucial to move toward this condition so that all conversations generated by feedback can point to one thing—student learning. The only questions about feedback that matter are, "Where is the student?" and, "How can the student reach the next level?" If feedback leads students to ask these kinds of questions of themselves and follow up with you about them, you should welcome those discussions with open arms—even if they are uncomfortable.

Keep it simple: Your marks (including feedback and grades) on a student's assessment should accurately and completely reflect the extent to which the assessment lines up with the standards presented in advance of the assessment. For example, if a history teacher has assigned an exercise wherein students need to summarize an article from *The Wall Street Journal*, she should mark it according to a clear set of expectations, previously conveyed to students, for the primary components of the summary. By isolating the components on a scale that indicates what excellent, good, fair, and poor performance look like, the teacher has removed assessment from a realm where it can be challenged or where its intent is unclear to the students. It must be clear to the students that they will be assessed based upon the articulation of specific skills and knowledge. And the teacher's feedback should indicate and suggest paths or strategies for improvement.

If and when students "complain" about their grades or feedback, you should be able to quickly move the dialogue into productive territory by simply going through the expectations and process used to mark the paper in the first place. The discussion becomes productive when the students and you begin to brainstorm ways in which they may more closely align their work with higher standards. These discussions also empower students with knowledge of the ways in which they may reach a higher mark.

Insight # 2

When handling assessments, we must plan our nonteaching time in relation to the way we want our students to interact with and process our feedback.

The second insight derived from my vignette speaks to the need to alter your typical classroom planning methods to make room for a concentrated examination (on the part of the students) of assessment data. You must not simply return assessments and allow students to run out of the classroom (or run out of the classroom yourself). As Rick Stiggins (2007) points out, students "make crucial decisions based on the [data we generate with our assessments]. In fact . . . the decisions they make as users of assessment results exert far greater influence on their success as learners than do the decisions made by the adults—the parents, teachers, administrators, and policymakers—around them" (p. 60). You must plan when the feedback will be most useful to instruction and student learning. Based on this plan, you can also structure the time when the actual marking of assessments will take place. Here's how:

When you collect a pile of assessments, open your plan book or whatever you use to sketch out the scope and sequence of your daily lesson plans. Ask yourself, Where will the feedback be most useful to students? Tomorrow? Three days from now? Students need quick and accurate feedback, but they don't necessarily need everything back all at once.

In addition, analyzing the timing of your feedback helps you to block out the time to grade assessments. Once you have determined where feedback fits in the daily unfolding of your curriculum, you are ready to schedule the time for the actual grading process. Mark this time expenditure in your daily calendar, being realistic about your grading capabilities. Some people can sit down and grade an entire stack of papers without moving. Others can only grade for twenty minutes at a time. Once you have figured out how much time the grading *should* take you personally, you can break up that time to suit your own habits. What's more, once this time is scheduled, no other appointments should interrupt that time. When you open your calendar on a given day, you know exactly when you will grade.

As you become more effective in executing this discipline (actually grading during the time you set aside for grading), you will have the distinct pleasure of not thinking about your grading all the time. Many teachers are haunted by the grading that piles up and are hounded by students who want to know "When will we get that test back?" Taking charge of your grading will allow you to keep the haunting and hounding at bay: you can tell yourself and your students exactly when it will be done.

Vignette 2

A few years later, and a bit more seasoned as a teacher, I remained pleased with the fact that I had ignored the first piece of assessment advice I had ever been given. Instead, I gave back my papers and tests early enough in each class to guarantee that students had a chance to look over them. I wrote long comments, corrected every mistake, and passed out scoring guides. I became increasingly curious, though, about what happened during that 5- to 10-minute reflection period after I instructed students to look over the assessment and take note of necessary improvements. I decided to insert a quick test into the next round of papers I passed back. In that batch, I wrote comments as I normally did, but I also inserted symbols. I had a key for the symbols (for example, a circle meant that a student had to rethink a statement, a triangle meant that a student had made an excellent point), but I did not pass out the symbol key to my students.

I was surprised by the response. The students didn't say a word. They reviewed their feedback, checked the grade (not necessarily in that order), and we moved on with the day's lesson. At the end of the period, 3 out of 16 students approached me. One had a question about his grade. The other two had questions about the meaning of the symbols and did not want to ask the question during class. I thanked them for noticing and asked them if they knew why no one else asked about the symbols. They candidly told me what I already suspected—most students simply cared about the grade. If it met their minimum criteria, that chapter of their lives was closed. If it did not meet their minimum criteria, they would dispute the grade if they thought it would matter or simply cross their fingers and hope their parents didn't get wind of it. One of the students then said, "Mr. V., you want the conversation to go on and on, but right now it's pretty one sided."

Insight # 3

Students have to be taught to value and use feedback.

Like the "mentor" teacher in my first vignette, some students have no interest in entering a feedback loop or conversation. They want to know their grade—and that's it. Once they learn their grade, they frequently see it as something that has been given to them rather than something they have earned. As a teacher, then, you have to engineer in advance the kind of relationship you want to engender between students and the feedback you give them. You have to structure these exchanges and foster an ongoing relationship between feedback and learning.

While thinking about a better way for students to use a five-minute reflection period after I return their assessments, I realized that students' understanding of the assessment process, like any other learning process, is diverse. Some students intuitively understand the process, while others require some coaching, and in some cases, even some coaxing. You can gauge a student's understanding of the process by compiling a simple set of questions and passing them out with your feedback and grades.

1. "Do you understand the terms used in my feedback?" (If you are assessing students' ability to write a thesis statement, and they do not know what the term *thesis statement* means, you cannot expect the students to know how to improve that aspect of their writing.)

2. "Does the feedback on your paper or test prepare you for the actual grade?"

3. "Discuss the relationship between the feedback provided and the grade earned." (Questions two and three give you feedback on how well you are communicating; they may also show you if your grading methods are transparent enough.)

4. "What aspect of this feedback process motivates you?"

5. "What aspect of this feedback process frustrates you?" (Questions four and five connect to motivation, which is an extremely important, impossible to quantify, aspect of the feedback process.)

Students should write a response to these questions, or a version of these questions, after each major assessment. Depending on your own workflow, you can ask students to submit their answers for your review, store their answers in an assessment portfolio for later review, or set up a brief conference with you to discuss their answers.

Another easy technique to ensure that students pay focused attention to your feedback is to give them the feedback first, and then give them their grades. You also can ask students to provide their own feedback and grade, and then compare it to your own. The challenge here is to invite students to be more than simply passive receivers of feedback and grades.

One final way to engender this kind of responsibility and classroom culture involves having students track their own progress with the feedback you provide on specific assignments. In his text *Classroom Assessment and Grading That Work*, Marzano (2006) advocates for an assessment process wherein students track their own improvement over time. He believes that "One of the most powerful and straightforward ways a teacher can provide feedback that encourages learning is to have students keep track of their own progress on topics" (p. 89). In the text I am referencing, Marzano also invites the use of a four-point scale that can help guide students in their efforts to chart their progress.

Having tried to pitch this method to teachers, I realize how difficult it is to convince people that they should avoid typical grades in favor of a four-point scale that can later be converted to a grade. They also balk at the notion of spending time teaching students how to chart their progress, preferring to use their time to teach students subject-specific skills and content instead. However, even if slightly watered down (the good, rather than the perfect), Marzano's recommendation has the potential to generate a shift in responsibility from teacher to student. For example, in a foreign language class, the teacher can facilitate students' engagement with assessment by giving them the chart in Figure 2.1 at the start of a semester.

Figure 2.1

Fill in your grades on each assessment.

Vocabulary 1 _____   Reading 1 _____

Vocabulary 2 _____   Reading 2 _____

Vocabulary 3 _____   Reading 3 _____

After three assessments in both categories, review your grades as well as your actual marked assessments. Establish a focus for an assessment conversation and set up a meeting with me.

Meeting date _____ time _____ place _____

The meeting will focus on:

_____

_____

_____

_____

_____

_____

_____

This resource helps students chart their progress, observe trends in their own work, and build responsibility as they set up and plan their own meetings.

Insight # 4

If we're not careful, our feedback will say more about us than it says to our students.

When my student spoke honestly to me about the one-sided nature of my feedback on assessments, she pointed out the thing I could not see: My feedback shined a light *on me*, not on my students. Earlier in this chapter, I mentioned a guiding principle: that we resist the urge to let the quest for perfection stamp out the appearance of the good. Another guiding principle, important for busy educators, is the need to interrogate the obvious in search of the possible.

What is most obvious and therefore most overlooked about feedback is that it is an act of communication. Like most communication, the granting of feedback is fraught with the possibility for misunderstanding, anger, confusion, and ill will. Stiggins (2007) reminds us that all the assessment data in the world are not worth a great deal if we do not "deliver [them] into the user's hands in a timely and understandable form" (p. 68). In short, our comments and grades mean nothing if students cannot use them.

Have you ever asked a colleague to try to make sense of a piece of student work that you marked? Better yet, have you ever asked a nonteaching friend to go through the same activity? When I have gone through this process, I have frequently heard reactions like, "You give a lot of comments. . . . I would find this kind of overwhelming. . . . I wouldn't even know where to start. . . . This looks like a Jackson Pollock painting." Not good.

Like many teachers, I have suffered from what Chip and Dan Heath (2007) call "The Curse of Knowledge" (p. 20). I teach writing, and as I recall, I taught myself how to write through a trial and error process that will probably continue for the rest of my life. In other words, when I teach writing, I am trying to guide students toward universal principles of good writing that I understand in a very personal, intuitive way. When I am grading quickly, as is often the case during the school year, I sometimes forget to think about what my students might think or not think, know or not know, when they read my comments. If I fail in presenting my feedback clearly, I have, in essence, failed as a communicator. According to the Brothers Heath, the road to recovery lies in taking the time to "readily re-create [my] listeners' state of mind" (p. 20). When writing comments on papers or tests, I have to think about my audience. What's more, I have to realize that my audience is comprised of a wide range of different students. Presumably, I cannot write to my failing student in the same voice I would use for my A student.

It's worth spending a bit more time with the Brothers Heath before wrapping up this point. In *Made to Stick,* the bestselling book I have been referencing, the Brothers Heath frequently mention teachers—but they do so only in the context of a teacher trying to communicate a difficult concept in a class. I tend to push their insights deeper into the educational field by applying their insights to the intimate exchange of feedback and grades that happens on a daily basis in schools across the country. Really, what could be a more important "sale" for teachers than the ideas, hints, and suggestions contained in their feedback? Which profession could be more in need of stickiness training than a profession that competes for the attention of the text-message–barraged, social-networked, video-gamed, hormone-bent minds of adolescents?

To make ideas stick, the Heath Brothers stickily present insights about storytelling, emotion, and credibility. Best for the purpose of providing feedback that sticks, though, are their insights on simplicity and surprise. When talking about simplicity, they encourage us to prioritize the message we want to convey: "To get at the core, we've got to weed out superfluous and tangential elements. But that's the easy part. The hard part is weeding out ideas that may be really important but just aren't the most important idea" (p. 28). For a teacher used to marking everything that needs attention, this presents a huge challenge. Do we really want to overlook the small-sized problems? The medium-sized problems? I would say yes and no. We may not be able to isolate a single piece of feedback, but we can seek to avoid overindulgent feedback—that is, feedback that simply overwhelms students rather than helping students clearly prioritize where they should put their efforts in order to reach the learning target for which they are aiming. We can learn to be strategic in our use of time, energy, and attention.

What's more, we can strive to write feedback in ways that are surprising to students. The Heath Brothers talk a lot about finding ways to break patterns. They contend that, by breaking a pattern, authors cause information to stand out to casual observers whose brains are wired to "be keenly aware of changes" (p. 65). The ideal feedback, it seems to me, would be unexpected in a way that connects to the simple, prioritized point, the specific learning goal.

My own triumphs with this kind of sticky feedback have happened when I managed to know my students well, to understand their strengths and weaknesses, and to think clearly about what they needed most. One memorable case involved a student who had severe issues with redundancy. After seeing this problem sink his grade on numerous assignments, I wrote him a half page response on the back of one of his papers. The response repeated the same point (about redundancy) over and over and over. I did not mention the four other, smaller mistakes he was making. To make a huge leap in performance, he simply needed to fix one critical piece of his writing. When he read my comment, he started laughing . . . and kept laughing about it for the next four years. His work improved tremendously, and I would bet that after my feedback, he thought about redundancy every time he sat down to complete a serious writing assignment.

Vignette 3

The final vignette in my grading trilogy came a few years later. During one of those strange moments of synchronicity that sometimes happen in schools, all the teachers I bumped into seemed to be a bit behind in their grading. We were approaching the midpoint in a semester, life was hectic as usual, and everyone was nursing a pile of assessments, trying desperately to get them back to their students. That week, people talked less and worked more, grade books filled up with numbers, students received their graded assessments, and the school machine churned ever closer to the midpoint of the year. Everything seemed fine. But then I started thinking about what we lose sometimes when we race to meet our own expectations and the standards of our profession.

Insight # 5

A pile of completed student assessments (i.e., quizzes, tests, papers) is an enormous ecosystem, informing us about how we taught, what we taught, what can be better, and where we need to go. If we do not intend to pay attention fully to these assessments, we should question the rationale for assigning them in the first place.

In his monograph *Good to Great and the Social Sectors*, Jim Collins (2005) urges us (workers in the social sectors) to "separate inputs from outputs, and hold [ourselves] accountable for progress in outputs" (p. 5). There are few clearer instances of inputs and outputs in school life than a pile of assessments. The inputs are our time when we prepare the assessment, plus the students' time when they prepare for and complete the assessment, plus our time when we grade the assessment. And the outputs are the student's answers or work, along with the feedback, grade, and any follow-up that occurs. Failure to study and make use of these outputs may be the single biggest waste of time and energy in the profession.

Too much time is wasted during grading because teachers do not gather data, other than grade data, while they are marking assessments. This means that they are unable to accurately measure improvement throughout the semester (or throughout the years). Imagine taking a bag of oranges and trying to make a pitcher of orange juice by only giving each orange a quick, light squeeze before discarding it. Time would pass, but you would only fill a single glass. Every time we sit down with a pile of tests or papers and simply derive a grade and a few comments, we have only filled a single glass. The glass may be delicious, and it may quench some of our thirst, but it will not feed an entire group of people—it will not feed a class.

Sadly, we have done the work anyway. We have spent the time. We simply deserve more robust productivity. We deserve a greater return on our time. Here are some suggestions:

• While you are grading, if you are lucky enough to have a computer by your side, open a Word document and an Excel spreadsheet. (If you cannot grade near a computer, use two blank pieces of paper.) Label the documents with the title of the learning targets presented in the assessment. As you mark the assessments, use the documents to record information that might help to drive your future classes.

• In the Word document, type in exemplary passages or solutions, passages or solutions that need corrections, passages or solutions that demonstrate creative answers or daring mistakes, passages or solutions that were right or almost right. This process will generate a class-specific document to pass out during your future lessons.

• In the Excel spreadsheet, keep track of the kind and number of errors made by each student. This process will generate a snapshot of a class's strong and weak points and give you a snapshot of each child. As the year moves along, you will begin to compile a historical database tracking the class progress as well as individual student progress.

Some researchers recommend that you go even further, organizing your entire grade book around benchmarks for learning rather than lists of scores categorized by types of assessments. Pollock (2007) points out the value of such a practice: "When teachers score by deconstructing an activity score into different benchmarks in the grade book, patterns emerge and become useful for describing the learner's performance, giving specific feedback about it, and making decisions about what to do next" (113). Regardless of whether you choose my scaled-down method or a method that inspires you to fundamentally revise your entire record-keeping process, you must build personal accountability into your assessment practice. Is the class making fewer errors in given categories? Are individual students progressing or falling behind? How do you know?

A FEW FINAL WORDS

Surely some of these strategies will fit neatly into your daily teaching and grading habits. I am not asking you to spend more or less time on assessment—only to make sure the time you do spend is all that it can be, all that it should be. Figure 2.2, following, will serve as a reminder of some of the key points presented in this chapter.

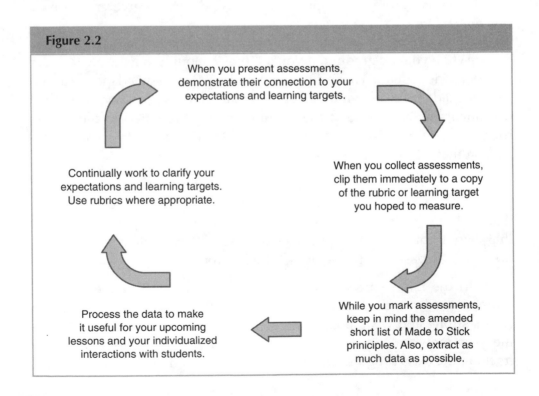

Figure 2.2

When you present assessments, demonstrate their connection to your expectations and learning targets.

When you collect assessments, clip them immediately to a copy of the rubric or learning target you hoped to measure.

While you mark assessments, keep in mind the amended short list of Made to Stick priniciples. Also, extract as much data as possible.

Process the data to make it useful for your upcoming lessons and your individualized interactions with students.

Continually work to clarify your expectations and learning targets. Use rubrics where appropriate.

Imperative 3

Hold Great Meetings Founded on Authentic Commitment

Teachers spend an awful lot of time in meetings. Think about it: faculty meetings, school meetings, department meetings, tricampus meetings, committee meetings, parent meetings, strategic-planning meetings, meetings to plan for other meetings—all in addition to our usual classroom meetings. As responsible professionals committed to continual improvement, we have to ask how can we maximize our own and other people's time in these various settings.

Let's start our consideration of meetings with a spine-straightening fact. If you attend a meeting with nine other teachers and it lasts an hour, 10 powerful resources have been removed from the students in your community. Those 10 teachers easily could have used that time to benefit students. They could have held student-teacher conferences to review student work, graded a substantial number of assessments that could give students prompt feedback, or donated SAT coaching to students in the community who cannot afford private tutors. That this list could go on for several more sentences, if not paragraphs, calls forth a sobering epigram: whenever a meeting is called, a deficit is born. Whether you are calling a meeting or attending one, then, you have a huge responsibility.

This chapter could well be called "Commitment." When you attend a meeting or run one, you have to leave a lot at the door—time, ego, your own agenda. At the end of a long sprint of a day, at the start of a long climb of a day, in the middle of a short lunch, in between phone calls, out from under huge stacks of papers, you have to find the extra energy to think hard about a problem, to contribute personal expertise or perspective, and to spend yourself for the hundredth time—for students.

WHY MEET?

We should not meet out of habit—because that's what we've always done. We should not meet simply because someone has the authority to call a meeting—and does. We should not meet to share information that is not pertinent or relevant. And we should not meet to loaf through an agenda that was simply generated to fill a scheduled meeting time.

A meeting, at its best, will be a natural convergence in response to a real need in the community. Is a particular kind of training needed? Does a particular problem need to be solved? Does a policy need attention? Has something bubbled up to the surface? The following urgencies underlie effective meetings; all are tied to the strengthening of collegiality on behalf of students:

- *The need to inform a decision or help someone solve a problem.* At times, individual teachers or administrators, due to the nature of their jobs, need to make final decisions on their own. This fact does not preclude them from hearing multiple perspectives. In fact, diversity of opinion and ideas will most likely lead to a better decision. As Stephen P. Robbins (2003) writes, "The evidence suggests that conflict can improve the quality of decision making by allowing all points, particularly the ones that are unusual or held by a minority, to be weighed" (p. 138).
- *The need to make a decision or solve a problem through a democratic process.* Some decisions are best left to a team, especially when those decisions affect the daily functioning of that team. Meetings can be called to help teams discuss important issues and then vote on a resolution.
- *The need to share relevant information with key members of the community.* Meetings spurred by information dispersal can be tricky and have a rather large penchant for failure. Often, the same goals can be accomplished with a memo. However, if the information is complicated, or you expect it to generate questions or discussions, a meeting should be called and a presentation

given. Moreover, if the information is highly sensitive, it might be better to discuss it with select members of the community rather than committing it to a memo that may be left out or facing up in a frequently used trash bin.

- *The need to build a foundation of trust that can serve as the basis for future work.* These days, we handle a lot of business over e-mail, but e-mail has limits. Getting together, actually meeting face-to-face, is an important act when e-mail becomes an interpretive zone rather than an informational exchange. Let's say you send an e-mail to a parent about the fact that his son is not doing his homework. You write a simple line: "John has not completed three out of the last six homework assignments, and this is hurting his grade." The parent quickly fires back: "Why didn't you tell me this two homeworks ago?" You write back, "I asked John to notify you." The parent writes, "John's fifteen. You're the adult. Don't you think you should step in, especially if he is 'hurting his grade?' Would you stand by and watch a child 'hurt' himself physically? Would you stand by if a student tried to 'hurt' another student? I expect stronger intervention in a school that advertises 'individual attention' in all its glossy brochures." At this point, another e-mail is worthless. The parent in this exchange is demonstrating his own analytical skills, his own facility with language, his own professional aptitude—and the child is still not doing his homework. It's time for a meeting in order to take the conversation out of the analytic, adult world and into a world where the student can begin to grasp his responsibility for completing homework assignments.

- *The need to delegate work or review delegated work.* The delegation meeting is very important for committees that have specific tasks. The facilitator has to clearly assign tasks and set a clear deadline for reporting. Asking people to report in front of a group is a great way to create accountability and build collegiality.

- *The need to build, refine, or examine the results of shared vision.* The shared-vision meeting is both a proving ground and a testing ground. At times, it allows groups of teachers to figure out a defining belief, a belief to guide their future actions. On the other end, it allows them to see how this belief plays out, giving them time and space to examine data or student work in light of the belief.

Running Meetings

Your job, when running meetings, is to avoid as much as possible the fuzziness that can mar a meeting's effectiveness. A good meeting has a clear objective, goes on only as long as is necessary, and ends with a clear assigning of tasks or parameters for follow-up. You should expect and encourage people to contribute, to stand up for their values, and to avoid neutrality.

Further strategies depend on the particular kind of meeting you are running and are discussed below.

Meeting With Teachers

When you are running a meeting with teachers, you have to think about results, relevance, and responsibility.

Begin by reviewing the urgencies listed above. Are you calling a meeting to solve a problem, to provide training for a perceived gap in teacher knowledge or skills, or to inform a particular swath of the community about an event that concerns them? If your results are aligned with a relevant urgency, the meeting will appear relevant to the teachers in attendance.

Responsibility, and your stance on responsibility, is tied to the preparation for and implementation of the meeting. It is also what separates good facilitators from mediocre facilitators.

Your stance on adults and responsibility defines the amount of responsibility you yourself will take for the success of your meeting. It's nice to assume that teachers are responsible, that they will mark all meetings on their calendars, prepare in advance for meetings, bring what you ask them to bring, show up on time, and shuffle conflicting appointments in advance.

But some teachers, for whatever reason, have trouble completing all these actions. As a meeting facilitator, you need to figure out how much you will do to compensate (or, depending on your point of view, overcompensate) for your team members' busy schedules. I have seen two models: one geared toward behavior modification and one geared toward success.

In the behavior-oriented model, the facilitator sends out the meeting agenda and requirements in advance, shows up at the meeting, takes attendance, and begins. As people show patterns of lack of preparation or absence, they are referred to the administration or removed from the group. I call this a *behavior-oriented model* because it seeks to modify the behavior of the people on the team by keeping track of things that they do not do.

In the success-oriented model, the facilitator takes a much more active role to ensure that the meeting has a positive outcome. He or she sends out an agenda *and* a reminder, brings extra copies of necessary materials, rounds up stragglers, encourages people to play active roles in the meetings (i.e., as presenters or note takers), and supports people as they seek to complete meeting-generated action items. I call this a *success-oriented model* because the facilitator works hard to establish the best possible conditions for a successful outcome (although by no means am I suggesting handholding professional, responsible adults who are not holding themselves accountable).

Based on what we know about the current rate of change in society, the success-oriented model seems to be right for our schools. In *The Age of Speed*, consultant and speaker Vince Poscente (2008) connects leadership style to the rate of change, highlighting John Kotter's "dichotomy between management and leadership" (p. 59). Management, Poscente writes, "is mostly concerned with the status quo, while leadership is tied to change" (p. 59). The behavior-oriented facilitator reacts to people's negative qualities, while the success-oriented facilitator ensures that people, even ridiculously busy people, have an opportunity to put their best feet forward. In a world marked by rapid increases in the speed at which we communicate, do business, and process transactions, groups that do not succeed quickly will be left behind. Figure 3.1 will help you to plan success-oriented meetings.

Accountability

Once you have demonstrated to your team members that you are a success-oriented facilitator, you also have to protect your energy. You can't do everything for everyone. If, in spite of your best efforts, you have meeting members who are perpetually unprepared, don't take it personally. Instead, take notes, gather some data, and at an appropriate point, bring the problem to their attention in a collegial manner. Ask them to get on board. Remind them why they are valued members of the team—what they have to offer. And if that doesn't work, remove them from the team.

Let's Not Forget the Students

Remember my earlier comment about the fact that every meeting creates a deficit? As you plan meetings, you must deliberately steer them in a direction that connects to students—student life, student achievement, student learning. When observing a student-centered meeting you might see or hear

1. Student work
2. Student data
3. Student names (if appropriate)
4. People advocating for students
5. Discussion of policies that affect student life

Figure 3.1

Planning the Success-Oriented Meeting

Meeting Title/Objectives:

Outcomes

Expected outcomes:

Relevance to the student body:

How will we reach the outcome:

Participants

Who needs to give input:

Who needs to be present:

Notes on group dynamics that might
need attention:

Facilitator Actions

I will send out the agenda via
e-mail/mail/other to:

Other required documents to be
e-mailed or delivered in advance:

I will send a reminder on:

I will provide the following
refreshments:

MEETING WITH STUDENTS (PART 1)

Speaking of students, you also should plan to meet with them from time to time—and you should plan these meetings carefully in order to ensure that they solve problems and address concerns. Too often, meetings with students end on a warm and fuzzy note. The student thinks she has accomplished something because she sat down with her teacher. The teacher feels like she has accomplished something too, because she spoke directly to the student, and perhaps the student was more attentive than usual. Perhaps the student could even demonstrate a clearer understanding of the material when the teacher walked her through it. It's not the warmth of this exchange that bothers me—it's the fuzziness.

If the meeting ends without a plan for action and follow up, if you're simply having a meeting because you don't know what else to do, or if you're simply having a meeting to appease an angry parent or fulfill an administrator's request, then you are wasting everyone's time.

We need to take a more systematic approach.

"Problem" Students

In Jane Pollock's (2007) book *Improving Student Learning One Teacher at a Time*, Gary Nunnally reflects on his experience with failing students:

> If my students were failing, they were not learning; and if they were not learning, it was my job to help them improve their learning! No longer could I think or say, "Well, if the student would just turn in his homework . . ." (p. 25)

Nunnally then goes on to discuss how Pollock's Big Four approach helps him to engage all learners in his classroom. Pollock's Big Four approach encourages teachers to use (1) precise terminology to describe what students will learn, (2) purposeful instructional planning and delivery, (3) purposeful assessment, and (4) deliberate assessment and feedback (p. 7). That's a terrific and vital approach, but we also need to turn an eye toward a teacher's work outside the classroom. After a meeting with a student, the student should leave with a specific action plan. The teacher, meanwhile, leaves with the duty to follow up with the student at a later date.

This method can be used with a range of students, but we'll start with the student who is in most need of our help. Some of the traditional responses to "problem" students are to send them to the principal, a psychologist or counselor, a tutor, or a learning lab, or to request a one-on-one meeting. How can a teacher know which approach to take?

Before reacting, I suggest that teachers reframe their notion of the problem student. The problem student is a "problem to be solved" student. Taking an analytic, problem-solving approach, one that is creative, student-centered, and systematic, helps to move teachers beyond what Mike Schmoker (1999) calls a "take my word for it" approach. Instead, it allows a teacher to exhaust all possibilities and hopefully discover a viable solution to the problem posed by the problem student.

Example 1: Problem manifested as behavior issue. If your problem student is misbehaving in class, set up a time to meet with him. After exchanging pleasantries, get to the point. Identify the specific action that is disrupting the class. Is the student talking out of turn? Being overly argumentative? Being cruel to another student? Once you have stated the problem, enlist the student to help you solve it. Sometimes students are not even aware of the behavior that is bothering you. Perhaps you can establish some kind of private sign that will notify the student when he is beginning to act in the specific inappropriate manner you have discussed. Or perhaps the student will tell you that he simply cannot stay focused, that he recently changed a medication, that he can't stop thinking about his parents' impending divorce. Perhaps the student needs to meet with a school counselor. Perhaps someone needs to call the student's parents and discuss the medication or the divorce. Perhaps the student needs a new seat in the class. I am generating this list to demonstrate the kind of specific thinking that is needed to solve problems in schools. But you must not stop at list generation.

The meeting is only halfway over once you have brainstormed a list of actions. From the list, with the student, select a next step. Make sure the step is specific. For instance, "I want you to talk to your parents this weekend about your medication. I will call them on Monday to follow up. We have to figure out why this new medication is causing you to act out in class." Or, "The next time you start to lose your temper in a discussion, I'm going to rub my nose. This will tell you that you are starting to exhibit the kind of behavior that I do not want to see. At that point, I want you to count to 10 before you reenter the discussion." Or, "I want you to set up a meeting with the school counselor. I want you to talk to her about the impending divorce. I will check in with her by next Friday."

Once you have selected a specific step, put it in writing. The student should leave the meeting with a plan (prescription) and a date to return to your office to see how the plan worked. He should know, in advance, how you will check for (measure) success. The date for the second meeting should be copied immediately into your plan book. That meeting is as important as your class schedule. You need to tend to your classes in order to teach your students. You need to tend to your problem students in order to ensure that you are able to teach the rest of your students. It is counterproductive to prioritize class time over the time you meet with a student who has a negative impact on that class time.

Example 2: Problem manifested as not turning in work. Let's say that your problem student is not turning in work, and this deficit is causing her to fail your class. Call a meeting with the student. Start the meeting by showing the student your grade book. Show her exactly how her lack of work is bringing down her grade and exactly how a new commitment to work will bring up her grade. Transparency, in this case, is extremely important. What kid wants to work toward something that is abstract, unattainable, or will benefit her "over the long haul" but not in the present? Once you have established what's at stake, explore a bit. Ask questions. Try to find out why this student is not doing her work. Perhaps she doesn't have a quiet place to study at home. Or perhaps a transportation issue causes her to leave for school so early that she goes home and falls asleep at her desk. If this is the case, generate some options. Perhaps the student can work in your office during her free period. Perhaps you can designate a classroom where she can work for an hour after school each day. Perhaps you can work with an administrator to assign her to more study halls. If you uncover an extreme lack of concern in the student, you may have to try a different tactic. Will a phone call to the parents help? What about a meeting with the college counselor, who can explain exactly how an F on a report card will affect the student's college options? Regardless, once you have established your action plan, you have to make sure you follow up.

Follow-Up: In both examples, the follow-up meeting is crucial. People respond to quick, positive results, and motivation is an important part of the learning process. As a teacher, you have to be able to show your problem student that his or her action plan is leading to something concrete. And if the action plan is not leading to something concrete, a new plan needs to be put in place.

In the follow-up meeting or meetings, allow the student to report back to you. (Did he or she complete the action plan established in the first meeting?) Then report back to the student. (Has anything changed in your grade book, in your perception, or in the perception of others?) These meetings do not have to last long. In fact, if you approach them with clear agendas, they should be short. If the results are moving in the right direction, the action should be continued. If not, you must return to the protocol established in the first meeting: What do you hope to accomplish? What action will the student take? How will you measure the result? When will you meet again?

THE SYSTEMATIC APPROACH

The narrative above reveals the bones of the systematic approach to student meetings that can ensure that those meetings have a clear outcome.

Before exposing those bones, I should add a few quick caveats. First, humanity is required. You should not simply apply this system as a one-shot, cure-all for all student woes. The system is a guide for improvisation. In the end, you want the results that the system promises, but you have to attach warmth, humor, energy, and friendliness—all the things that motivate students in the first place. Second, this approach takes time. You are trying to solve problems so that they stay solved, and you do not have to return to them, or suffer their consequences, again and again. Third, one of your goals in using a system like this is to help the student internalize what amounts to little more than a commonsense, problem-solving process. When possible, use questions to spur students to think through the steps and draw their own conclusions.

Figures 3.2 and 3.3 will help you to plan and follow through on student meetings.

MEETING WITH STUDENTS (PART 2)

Over the course of my career, I have noted a curious fact: my strongest students set up the most meetings with me. Perhaps this is not so curious, though. They understand how to advocate for themselves and enjoy the company of teachers, since teachers always have been viewed as allies for and facilitators of their success. In a meeting with a strong student, you can use the system described above, but in many cases, you will have difficulty measuring or following up on progress because all signs may already point to exceptional work. One of my favorite questions in education is, How do you improve on an A (or an A+, depending on the highest score in your grade range)?

The other grouping of students is the "middle student," or the student who flies below the radar. This student is not doing so poorly that the alarm sounds. At the same time, he or she is not seeking additional

Figure 3.2

Isolate the Problem

Step 1

Talk to the student, put him or her at ease, thank him or her for coming, and explain what you hope to accomplish or ask him or her what he or she hopes to accomplish.

Step 2

Isolate the problem that needs to be solved. You can either coach the student to identify the problem or you can explain the behavior that is causing the problem. (Remember the lesson beneath the lesson—you are teaching kids how to think about, frame, and solve problems.)

Step 3

Brainstorm strategies to solve the problem. These should be specific actions that can be implemented. Try to develop a fairly long list.

Develop a Solution

Step 4

Pick one strategy after talking through their merits.

Step 5

Develop a plan for implementing the strategy. The plan should include (a) when and where the action or strategy will start, (b) an explanation of how you both will know if the strategy is working, and (c) deadlines for checking progress.

Step 6

Write a prescription. It's a good idea to ask the student to write the prescription at the end of the meeting to make sure he or she has internalized the information.

Figure 3.3

Post-Meeting Prescription

Date _____

What's wrong? Why did we have a meeting today?

_____

_____

What strategies did we discuss?

_____

_____

Which strategy did we choose?

_____

_____

When and where will the student begin to implement the strategy?

_____

_____

How will we know if the strategy works?

_____

_____

When will we meet again? _____
What do I need to bring to the follow-up meeting?

_____

_____

What do you need to bring to the follow-up meeting?

_____

_____

challenges. He or she simply wants to earn midrange grades and be left alone. And, as busy professionals, teachers sometimes enter an unspoken (or unconscious) pact to allow these students to coast. After all, they don't disrupt classes or complain, and their parents often do not complain either. Everything's fine.

This is a great place to dig in, to reach out to kids and challenge them, even if they're not quite happy about it. Teachers are tested and become exceptional in the ways they respond to the everyday challenges of school—the ordinary, not the extraordinary, and how they teach each student, each day. At the end of your career, will you be able to say you helped your lowest achieving students solve their problems? Did you model for them an effective, honest approach to confronting their limitations? Did you look at an A+ student and find room for improvement, even though it could not be factored into a grade? Did you fight through the complaisance (your own, your student's, and even your school's) surrounding the middle student?

MEETING WITH PARENTS

Although you won't always feel like you are "running" a parent meeting, and the facilitator's role will often shift between the parent and you, you can still walk into a parent meeting with some strategies.

Parent meetings happen for a variety of reasons: a parent wants to talk about a student's grades, your grading system, your treatment (real or perceived) of his or her child, a program and why his or her child is or is not recommended for it. A parent wants something to happen or doesn't want something to happen. A parent wants to give you some important, sometimes confidential information about his or her child—possibly in an effort to help you understand the child's needs. Regardless of the reason, parent meetings are very rarely called as an out-and-out celebration of the teacher . . . and they are very often a point of stress for teachers. Figure 3.4 offers a flexible template for how to run a meeting that you aren't necessarily running.

Focus and name. If possible, give the meeting a name before it even begins. If a parent contacts you and asks to set up a meeting, try to ferret out the purpose of the meeting. This will allow you to do your homework and bring the necessary data to the table. It also will give the meeting some rough parameters and, therefore, a projected outcome, allowing you to keep the meeting on track. For example, if a parent comes in to talk about his child's homework record and in the middle of the meeting he begins to

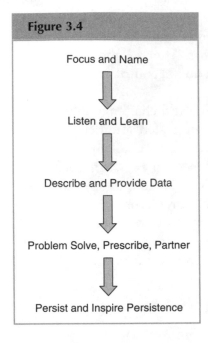

Figure 3.4

Focus and Name

Listen and Learn

Describe and Provide Data

Problem Solve, Prescribe, Partner

Persist and Inspire Persistence

talk to you about problems with another teacher, you can easily refocus the meeting by saying, "I hear what you are saying, but let's solve the homework problem in my class, first. If we have time left over after that, we can return to the other issue or figure out a time and place to address it."

By focusing and naming the meeting, you also have the opportunity to consider whether the child would benefit from taking part in the discussion. Sometimes a parent will make this decision for you, wanting to meet with or without the child, but at other times, the parent will be looking to you for guidance and defer to your recommendation. In any event, it's worth putting it on the table for the parent to consider. Often, adults can wrap up a problem and put a beautiful bow on it, but the solution that seems so clear and direct to the adults seems impossibly muddled to a 15-year-old. If the student is present, he or she can begin to take ownership of the problem and its solution in a language he or she can understand.

Listen and learn. Understand that a parent's job is to love and advocate for his or her child. Parents and teachers may be operating with very different assumptions about what is best for a particular child, and as a result, they may not agree on the best way to care for a particular child. For example, while some parents feel the need to "cover" for their children, sheltering them from some of the pressures of high school, a teacher might feel that the child's inability to take responsibility for his or her actions is the root of the problem. This disparate view is an unspoken part of the process, something we would never consciously address in a meeting.

So listen. Pay attention not only to words but also to actions. And then listen some more. Your primary job in a parent meeting is to learn as much as you can about the child in question. Parents often, not only in their words but also in their demeanor, reveal important details that will help you understand the child about which you are meeting. In my experience, even if a parent is extremely frustrated, extremely emotional, or extremely rude, you can ascertain something that will help you in your effort to help the child. I'm not suggesting that you calmly submit to a verbal lashing. Remember, if you feel uncomfortable, you can always end a meeting by saying, "I'm really not comfortable with your tone, so I'm going to suggest that we reschedule this meeting, and I'm going to ask my boss to sit in on it."

I am suggesting, however, that you remain firmly committed to the child being addressed in the meeting. You might learn that a child is not sleeping properly, that a child is dealing with bullying or abuse, or that a child is living through a nasty divorce. Or you might learn that a student is balancing a ridiculously complex ballet schedule, nurturing a growing interest in photography, or trying out for an AAU basketball team. This is information you can use in your daily interaction with students as you attempt to hook them to the learning process. In a blog on *The New York Times* website, Errol Morris (2008), a groundbreaking documentary filmmaker, writes, "[We] assemble our picture of reality from details. We don't take in reality whole. Our ideas about reality come from bits and pieces of experience. We try to assemble them into something that has a consistent narrative" (para. 8). A good teacher, like a good reporter or filmmaker, knows the power of the revelatory, almost magical detail. Think about your best relationships with students. Surely, some of them blossomed because of little details along the way. Perhaps you started talking about a trip the student took over the summer, a film the student likes, or a sport's team the student avidly follows. You have to grab these details wherever you can find them, and parents are a great resource.

Describe and provide data. After listening to the parent—whether the parent is calm or upset, demanding answers or seeking advice—without judgment or interpretation, you have to deliver two sets of information. First, you have to describe what the student has done or not done. Then you have to explain the expected target. For example, if a student has been rude or disrespectful in class, quote, as accurately as possible, what was said or what happened. Then explain the expected standard of behavior and how that standard was presented to the students. Likewise, if a student earned a failing grade on a paper, produce the paper, produce the rubric or scoring guide, and explain in precise terms why the paper does not reach the expected targets. Also helpful, in the latter case, is to provide samples of excellent, good, and fair responses to the assignment.

Once you have this information on the table, the parent may want to enter the conversation—sometimes forcefully—by explaining a student's motive or the way you may have misinterpreted a given situation. Motives aside, you must let the parent know that you have simply described what happened or failed to happen, and now you want to figure out how to fix the problem.

In many cases, the parents may think the problem is you. Stone, Patton, Heen, and Fisher (2000), in *Difficult Conversations,* advise us to "reframe" difficult situations by "taking the essence of what the other person says and 'translating' it into concepts that are more helpful" (p. 202). So, you remove "you" from the equation by returning to the plain description of the student's work or behavior and the objective standard or target. You reframe the conversation by (1) explaining that you are willing to do whatever you can to help the student reach the standard or target and (2) moving the conversation into a problem-solving mode.

Problem solve, prescribe, partner. You're the professional, so act like it. Once, after feeling flu-like symptoms for a few days, I went to a doctor, described what was ailing me, in detail, and he said, "so what do you make of all this . . . what do you think is wrong?" I left the office and found another doctor who was willing to take the facts and make a call. The second doctor wasn't one hundred percent sure in his diagnosis, but he named the problem and provided a solution to see how my body would react. That activity would provide him with additional data, moving us one step closer to a cure. Fortunately, his solution worked, and I was back on my feet in a few days. In your discipline, you should be like the second doctor, knowing your content and how to solve problems related to the delivery and reception of your content. In short, you should know, or be in the process of learning, relevant theories about how the brain learns, about methods of instruction, and about assessment.

Once you have presented your diagnosis of the problem and your prescribed solution, bring the parent on board. In terms of exigency, what can the parent offer? A quieter place to study? Helping the student review his or her homework log on a nightly basis? Fixing a printer that always breaks right when a major paper is due? Structuring a student's at-home Internet use? In terms of follow-though, what do you both need from each other? When can the parent expect a phone call from you? When can you expect a phone call from the parent? What constitutes progress, and how will both parties know when progress is or is not happening? What deadlines or check points can be established? These types of question will serve as the glue for the emerging partnership.

Persist and inspire persistence. A key concept to introduce in a meeting with a parent is persistence. That the student, teacher, and parent will have to persist in their efforts to affect change, keeping their sights clear throughout that process, is a given. In some cases, we cannot expect immediate results. For example, it could take an entire year for an unorganized child to gain a little bit of clarity and order in his or her life (let alone your class). So, reality is an important component of a good meeting. Most fixes in the complicated world of education require persistence. If parents leave a meeting thinking that everything will be easy and smooth, you might be seeing them again, and they might be less happy the second time around. Promise only what you can deliver, and remind parents of the importance of their contributions.

ATTENDING MEETINGS

Most teachers attend more meetings than they run. And most teachers, even the most collegial, complain from time to time (or even more) about meetings. That's not necessarily a bad sign. Teachers teach, and they should want to teach more than anything else they do in the school building. Anything that takes them from their teaching should be viewed skeptically.

The previous suggestions in this chapter help meeting leaders set the course for a productive meeting. But the people who attend the meetings, the same people who complain about meetings, are also responsible for the outcome of the meeting. A terrific softball game can be set up in a fabulous venue with all the requisite equipment, but if people show up without really wanting to break a sweat, the game that follows will hardly be worth the time.

The relationship among meeting participants needs to be dynamic, exciting, and synergistic. Sometimes the participant members of a meeting need to sprint ahead of the facilitator, suggesting new directions; sometimes the facilitator needs to rein in the participants, refocusing the task. Remember, the primary purpose of a meeting is to generate better results than could be produced by the effort of a single person working solitarily. You should not attend meetings; you should intend meetings. That is, your contribution to meetings should be geared toward producing a result. As a frequent facilitator of meetings, I cannot live without the following kinds of behavior, present in the very best colleagues I have known over the years.

1. Willingness to do the hard thinking—the most intangible item on my list, this is also the most important.

2. Preparedness—the best meeting participants have what they need, have thought about the meeting in advance, and have taken care of conflicting obligations so that they can concentrate on the meeting from start to finish.

3. Ability to ask probing follow-up questions or reframe questions in order to make sure everyone understands a task—in a good meeting, clarity is everyone's business.

4. Close reading—during discussions of policy or correspondence, the close readers are invaluable in their ability and willingness to analyze word choice, syntax, and rhetorical effect.

5. Toggling between micro- and macroviewpoints—every decision that is made has a ripple effect. Meeting participants who keep this in mind ensure good decisions. They ask, "What will this decision do to the student or students, the classroom, the program, the school?" "Is this event happening on the best possible date?" "How will it affect other events?"

6. Respectfully disagreeing—to have integrity, a group cannot always agree. In fact, continual agreement without debate or disagreement is a sign of groupthink, which can be quite harmful to an institution, especially in a time of rapid change.

7. Asking for evidence—our meetings need to be tied to reality. If not, they will never affect meaningful change. Evidence that stems from real school events should always have a place at our meeting tables.

8. Valuing something and standing up for it—if you support a certain aspect of the school, if you have a personal mission centered on what you think is best for students, if you are passionate about a particular program or policy, you need to stand up for it during meetings. In an effective school community, all voices are represented. If you are committed to education, indifference is not an option. There's too much at stake. You shouldn't necessarily want your argument to "win." Instead, you should want the best option to emerge from a healthy, well-played volley of ideas. And as Susan Scott (2004) writes about vice presidents of companies: "Some people . . . may be brilliant, but disappointingly (and irritatingly), they neither fish nor cut bait, they are neither hot nor cold. They appear to be, at best, politely indifferent" (p. 16). Don't be like those people.

9. Volunteering and following through—at good meetings, much is delegated. If you are handling a task for the group and you follow through on that task, you validate the work of the whole group, and you move the group forward.

10. Taking quality control personally—in a standing meeting, if something is not working, take responsibility by talking to the facilitator. Perhaps there is an unproductive pattern of participation where everyone is not equally heard. Perhaps the tasks have

appeared fuzzy or irrelevant. Perhaps people have other issues on their mind, and these issues are not seeing the light of day. You have a stake in the success of every meeting you attend.

DISTRACTIONS AND DISTINCTIONS

There are plenty of newfangled distractions for meeting facilitators and participants. Surely you've been in a meeting with people who are checking e-mail, receiving cell phone calls, texting, grading—in short, with people who demonstrate through their actions that they do not want to be there or that they are not committed to being "all there" the entire time. Then again, if a meeting is not relevant, why is it happening? Perhaps people should do other things. The old chicken and egg question can be applied to meetings. Do we unplug from meetings because they are irrelevant, or do meetings become irrelevant because we are not plugged in?

Regardless of how you slice it, meetings are bolstered by team players who enjoy a lively debate, who argue well and passionately on behalf of students, and who have healthy relationships in the community that, like muscles during weight training, are blissfully exhausted and concomitantly strengthened by the right amount of resistance. In fact, this kind of community, if it can be established, should often have another kind of meeting, one involving good food and drink to celebrate the simple fact that its members are helping each other grow as teachers and human beings.

Plato's "Allegory of the Cave" is worth thinking about before we stop thinking about meetings. Bad meetings leave us in the dark, looking at shadows on the wall. The shadows are mere imitations of reality, of real students and real school. Great meetings bring us, as a community, into the light. As we grapple with reality, there's sure to be a little pain, a little sensitivity to the light. But, for a school to be great, we need to build up a healthy tolerance for reality. We need to be authentic in our commitment to ourselves and to our schools. Having great meetings is a school habit, one that can and must be developed.

Imperative 4

Use Records to Generate Intentional Learning Opportunities

Think about your best school days from the past year. Surely they contained some great activities, solid decisions, evidence of learning, and exciting discoveries about the craft of teaching. Now think about your worst school days. They were probably riddled with poor decisions, weak lessons, and mistakes in judgment. More than memories, both the best and the worst days (and all days in between) contain the real work of teaching—work that can be saved, expanded, and improved. With a solid paper-based or paperless filing system comes a great opportunity to revisit the past and grow as a professional. Record keeping is not glamorous, but it provides the mechanism needed to shape a meaningful, deliberate career. Done well, it provides the evolving benchmark for your own achievement as a teacher. And by keeping accurate files and noting the documents that are placed in those files, teachers can enter a dynamic cycle of positive individual growth and continue to spark their students over the years.

THE EVERGREEN SYSTEM

Adopting a simple system for processing your work product (both what you produce and what you receive) can help you earn dividends on the original energy invested in that work product. I am *not* encouraging you to recycle the same documents year after year. Instead, I want you to renew and revise your documents so that they retain a state of being useful and exciting—evergreen—for each cycle of new students. You may need to update data or facts, modify examples, relate themes to the lives of particular students, or rethink the delivery based on new research about how students learn. Whether you use the revised document or throw it out in favor of starting from scratch, it is beneficial to have had it as a reference in the first place.

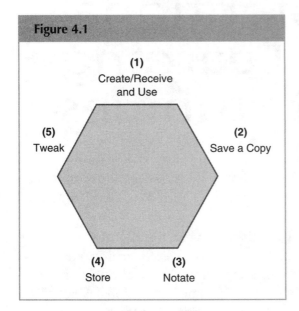

Figure 4.1

(1) Create/Receive and Use

(5) Tweak

(2) Save a Copy

(4) Store

(3) Notate

At the start of a teaching career, it's easy to feel like you are shouting down a long hallway. The echo seems to run away from you until it peters out and disappears. After a few years, though, a teaching career should feel more like a conversation—with the work of others and with your own work. Every document you create or collect can pass through a simple system, ensuring it an appropriate shelf life (Figure 4.1).

The rest of this chapter elaborates on each step in the system.

What You Create and Receive

As a teacher, you are asked to be a veritable cottage industry. Nearly everyday, you think of, write, or organize information. Alternatively, you comment on someone else's thinking, writing, or organization. You collect data or make meaning of statistics. You tell stories, give lectures, make presentations, prepare slideshows, and orchestrate activities. You describe and prescribe, you level without fully leveling, and you motivate. All this adds up to countless syllabi, handouts, assessments, directions, directives, notes, PowerPoint presentations, websites, e-mails, memos, letters, progress reports, videos, rubrics, and feedback.

Meanwhile, as you create, you receive. You receive e-mail from colleagues, parents, and students. You receive letters, memos, and instructions. You collect papers, quizzes, tests, projects, homework, and journals. You read blogs, websites, newspapers, scholarly journals, books, and listservs. You attend conferences.

In fact, if you decided on a Monday morning to simply stack up all the documents that you create or receive in a given week, you would end the week with a gigantic pile, filled with every possible educational transaction.

What's Worth Saving

Not all documents that cross your desk need to enter the Evergreen System. So, what documents that you create or receive on a daily basis *are* worth saving? How can you make sure that these documents will be saved in such a way that they are both accessible in and relevant to your future teaching practice? Failure to make judgment calls about what to keep and what to recycle is the equivalent of planting a garden but refusing to weed it.

Save honest work, done well. One rule, perhaps the number one rule, of effective practice is to do things right the first time. Spending an extra five minutes proofreading a complicated handout, finding and listing the sources of images used in a PowerPoint, writing your own model of a perfect sample for assessment: these small acts of concentration and discipline produce work that is worth saving. I know this rule sounds almost absurdly open-ended, but honest work, done well, can and should trickle down your career. The rule snaps into focus, too, if you think about what you will not keep—anything rushed, garbled, inaccurate, or patched together from a variety of different sources without citation.

Save student work and data. You should save student work for two reasons. First, student-produced documents are the artifacts of your job. These serve as a necessary reminder that you are building something and that your work adds up to something. Second, it provides excellent fodder for future lessons.

But you can't save every piece of student work, so you need to think in advance about what will be most valuable to your future lessons, your future students, or future developments in your classes. In particular, you might look for the types of samples listed in Figure 4.2.

Figure 4.2

What	Why
Work that demonstrates a common error	Every discipline has errors that pop up in each new class. Sharing examples of these errors in context, and asking students to correct them, is a great exercise. It raises student awareness and gives them practice in spotting mistakes in their own work.
Work that demonstrates an interesting or unique problem or risk	Educators talk all the time about productive risk taking and intellectual daring, but these phrases can sound like empty rhetoric to students who come to feel that every step of their high school careers must be perfect. Sharing real examples of student risk taking shows other students what is possible.
Work that is excellent, good, and fair	Having a tiered set of samples on any important assignment is useful for differentiation. Showing a failing student an example of a middle range paper is more encouraging than showing him or her a sample of a perfect paper.
Work that shows notable creativity or insight	Dan Pink's (2006) *A Whole New Mind* has been inspiring educators for a few years. He describes a world where creativity can lead the way. But, like any other skill or technique, students benefit from seeing examples. Telling a class to "be more creative" might not mean anything to many of the students, especially if they have been implicitly trained to seek "the right answer."

Aside from the physical work product, you also can save other student data, and I encourage you to be creative as you think about ways that your records might inform your future work. For example, at the end of a school year, you might want to run a quick correlation between final grades and homework grades, between final grades and absences, or attendance at extra help sessions and final grades. When you are speaking to next year's class or next year's parents, you can give them some hard numbers about the connection between student effort (on homework, in coming to school, etc.) and students' final grades. Although this information should never be offered as a guarantee of high grades, it is valuable from a counseling standpoint. You can tell constituents, "Take my word for it, I've studied the results." Longer term, you might compile records of a class of students, looking at how they perform on a grammar test in eighth grade and a similar test in ninth grade. You might look at a 10-year pattern of math scores in your class and examine how these scores relate to SAT scores during that 10-year period.

Given our current pace of school and life, it's hard to argue against a practice that offers to make meaning where before there was none. For a good primer on data and correlations, see Theodore B. Creighton's (2007) *Schools and Data: The Educator's Guide for Using Data to Improve Decision Making.*

Save when red flags tell you that you must. In the litigious-minded world in which we live, most teachers will face a situation where they have to answer questions about a specific student, situation, or grading practice. It is imperative for you to have written records, information, and reports regarding the particular situation, issue, or student. Otherwise, you will have to spend an enormous amount of time and energy trying to backtrack and find information to support yourself.

You can and should develop your own list of red flags throughout your career. Below are some examples of situations that should trigger red flag record keeping.

- You have to contact the student's parent or advisor.
- You have to remove a student from class.
- You have to give a student more than two detentions in a semester or quarter.
- A student's grade drops one full letter grade.
- A student seems to be upset with you.
- A student challenges your authority.
- A student questions your fairness.
- A student cheats in your class.
- A student has an accident in your class.
- Your gut tells you that something is just not right.

In the above examples, your records should include your notes, with dates, about your interactions with the student; e-mails from, to, or about the student; and samples of the student's work when appropriate. Chances are, you won't ever have to use these records, but if you are called to discuss a particular interaction or grading pattern, you'll be glad you can simply reach for a file.

Save things that truly matter. Grades, attendance, disciplinary infractions . . . these things are easy to record, and all teachers keep track of them in one way or another. But taking seriously for a moment the concept that "you get what you measure," it is clear that our records must be robust and varied. If we only measure grades, attendance, and disciplinary infractions, chances are we will create a lowest-common-denominator student. That is, we stand to create students who are only interested in their grades, who show up just enough to get credit, and whose moral and behavioral decisions are based on a quick calculation of whether or not their actions will lead to a swift reprimand from an authority figure.

Like a basketball coach who keeps an expanded stat book to keep track of players who dive for loose balls, take charges, tip the ball during a rebound attempt, or block shots without sending the ball out of bounds, we must challenge ourselves to keep records of things that are difficult to record, and we should use those records to inspire authentic progress.

An expanded grade book for a teacher might include categories such as the following:

- Asked a strong opening question
- Asked excellent follow-up questions during a discussion
- Welcomed a visitor into the class
- Supported a classmate
- Worked well in a group
- Took a strong, unpopular stance based on personal conviction

If this seems too detailed or limiting for you, I suggest you keep a notebook or journal about students in which you keep track of progress, significant anecdotes, and areas in which individual students struggle. This notebook certainly will come in handy when and if you are asked to write recommendations for students, meet with a parent, or simply help a student improve.

Save correspondence. If you have the network space, I recommend you save your e-mails going back at least three years. These e-mails should be categorized into subfolders within yearly folders (June to June).

When you save e-mails, you create a record of facts, decisions, and dates. Using your e-mail program's search and sort features, you can leverage e-mail as a tool for inquiry when questions are asked. For example, with my current e-mail records, I can tell you when and why my department adopted a new grammar book that hasn't worked very well, copy and paste an interview schedule for a job candidate from 2006 in order to use it for a job candidate in 2009, or pull some quotations from a nice e-mail I wrote about a freshman who is now a senior in need of a last-minute recommendation. Like your red-flag records, e-mail is a record that you will value when a specific question is posed.

HOW TO STORE AND USE RECORDS

Storing and using records involves two fundamental steps: notation and filing. Notation is particularly important because it reminds teachers about what worked, what didn't work, and what might change in specific lessons or assessments. If you're going to take the time to store a record, you should make it future-ready by marking it in some way. When you grab a document in a hurry next year or the year after that, how can you ensure that you will be able to quickly make sense and use of it?

I suggest that during its use or immediately after its use, you write in the margin of your document using a shorthand notation (in fact, you might tape the following list to your desk):

1. Worked perfectly

2. Did not work for some of the weaker students

3. Bored my stronger students

4. The circled sections need to be reworked completely

5. Students needed more background information

6. Great sample for students making the following mistake:
    _____

7. Great example of creativity

8. Good sample of student work

9. Fair sample of student work

10. Best of the year

If you are storing electronic copies of documents, that's even better. You can type right into the document (using bold or colored fonts), and when you open the document next year, you will know exactly how to modify it.

As you notate, you need to store, which means you need to think about space and time, the key elements at the heart of a good storage system.

A teacher's desk can quickly turn into a series of misshapen piles. As the week rushes on, the piles wobble and grow. Then Friday comes, and many teachers are so tired that they rush out of the building as if they have committed some kind of crime there. So the piles never really get processed. They simply will be pushed aside the next week and may be glanced at, trimmed, or purged from time to time.

As a first bastion of defense against unruly piles, set up processing stations using trays or labels. I have a tray for each class I teach, the committees I run, my club, and my advisees. As paper comes in, I notate it and throw it in its appropriate place. Then, I set aside time every month to file the paper. This isn't the best system (in the best system, you would file immediately), but it gives me just enough structure in just enough time to skate along the edge of organization, even on my busiest days.

When you are ready to file, hopefully you will not have to travel far. Your filing cabinet should be in your office or very close to your office. It should include anything that has been used and is ready to be stored. The primary reason for airtight filing is tied directly to a teacher's time. Teaching is an organic art. It builds off the work teachers have done in the past. Teaching is also a collaborative art. Teachers share material in order to build bridges between classes. Without effective files, teachers cannot access fully the work they have done in the past, and they cannot share with their colleagues.

Going Paperless

Not every teacher is ready to eliminate paper altogether, but it's not a bad idea. With a simple scanner, a computer, and a trusted backup drive, most documents can be converted into a digital format and stored in files that can be managed and accessed easily. Additionally, online teaching environments like Moodle or Blackboard allow teachers to build a master repository of class information, including teacher-created documents, websites, images, and video clips. With each new semester, teachers can select the items they will use or not use, tailoring course content to meet the needs of a new group of students. If you plan to save your life's work on a computer, though, you have to invest in an appropriate backup device such as an external hard drive or an online backup system, and you have to develop the habit of regularly backing up the contents of your computer.

Time—Short Term

As mentioned in Chapter 3, teachers attend a lot of meetings, and teachers play a key role in ensuring that those meetings are sites for exciting and important student-centered work. Your records also play an important role in meetings, and I recommend you create "working folders" for any committees of which you are a member, any projects on which you are working, or any meetings you have to attend or run. Every e-mail, every scrap of paper, every stray idea written on a sticky note that pertains to an individual committee, project, or meeting should go into its appropriate folder. (Note: if you have decided to go paperless, stickies and other notes should be quickly converted to a "memo to file" e-mailed to yourself, from yourself, and saved in the appropriate file.) Moreover, if you are the one running the meeting, you can simply pull the folder, or access it on your computer, before the meeting and use its contents to create an agenda.

Maintaining working folders allows a teacher to stop on the dime and head for a meeting. If pressed for time, all you have to do is grab (or access) the appropriate folder and spend a minute or two looking over it. You will then be ready to make a contribution. You also can reference the materials during the meeting if you have a physical file, or you print information for a meeting from your paperless file. This system of short-term record keeping maximizes your contribution and ensures essential information and ideas are not lost.

Time—Mid Term

The meeting input goes in folders, but the documents generated in meetings or committees should be stored in binders or in electronic folders on your computer. Binders and electronic folders allow for and indicate growth over time, a record that chronicles decisions or discussions from meeting to meeting and information that must be referenced in its entirety to track progress on a particular goal.

Time—Long Term

At some point, when the work in the binder is done, you may want to store its contents in a filing cabinet or archive it on your computer. By doing this, you build your own private research library. You can use it to answer questions such as, What did I do last year when I taught on the Great Depression? Did it work? Why did my calendar committee decide to change the date of graduation? What long-term trends emerged in my student grades? How did I handle parent X when I worked with an older sibling? What, specifically, can I say about one of my memorable students who now needs a recommendation for a college internship?

You will have to experiment with what works best for your files. I have tried several different methods, first filing based on broad categories like English 1, Satire, AP Literature, English Department, Literary Magazine, and so on. But these individual files swelled so much and so quickly that they became useless. I still ended up wasting a lot of time when I needed to find a particular piece of paper or to reference a previous lesson or article.

My current filing system is much more itemized. Like David Allen (2001) recommends, every new topic gets its own file. So, for example, if I teach a new book, it has its own file. Specific units in grammar have their own file. Departmental initiatives have their own file. Each club has a new file each year. The trick to making this kind of highly detailed filing system work is to create an index of files on your computer. As you add a new file, add its name to your index. In one quick glance, you can scan the entire contents of your filing system.

For those teachers interested in converting to a paperless filing system, document retrieval is even easier. After scanning your documents, saving them, and grouping them in relevant folders, you can easily access them.

Take it from Bill Gates (2006, April 7), who sang the praises of the desktop search in an article for Fortune magazine:

> Instead of having to navigate through folders to find that one document where I think a piece of information might be, [desktop search allows me to] simply type search terms into a toolbar and all the e-mails and documents that contain that information are at my fingertips. The same goes for phone numbers and e-mail addresses. (para. 16)

The wonderful thing about being organized (in the way I am describing in this chapter) is that it allows you to feel confident in your decisions, your conversations about students, and your correspondence. As your files grow over a career, they become a historical reference point. Is an A in your class the same as it was five years ago? What has changed, and why? Is an A in your class the same as an A in another teacher's class, when that class has the same description and serves the same level of students? How are your students doing in comparison to other students in the same grade? The act of keeping records will not make you a perfect teacher; as you start a year or unit, however, it will give you a real starting point, a benchmark, rather than a starting point that you simply snatch out of the air.

WHEN TO PURGE RECORDS

Your files can become so exhaustive that they are unmanageable, and from time to time you will have to set aside a few hours to recycle information that is no longer needed. You should eliminate any class handouts that start to feel dated or that simply lose their efficacy in a class setting. If you slip into the habit of simply reusing most of your old handouts or letters, you are on the cusp of disaster, and you are developing a very bad habit anyway. Remember, each time you touch an old document, you should seek to refresh it or recreate it—reimagine it in the context of a new class, a new parent body, a new school year, or a new era of education. If you can't do that, chuck it.

RECORD KEEPING AND DELIBERATE CHOICE

I want to leave you with a vision of a perfect teaching moment based on the principles in this chapter.

Vignette 1

You've been teaching for a few years or many (it doesn't matter) and keeping good records of your teaching. You have a great class, a truly memorable class, and you are planning to teach one of your all-time favorite units. You pull out (or access, if you've gone paperless) your file for the unit, and it has five different lesson plans, six different assessments, 12 samples of relevant student work covering a range of achievement levels. You have handouts, videos, student-made movies, bookmarks of websites, and so on. And everything in the file is carefully notated. You open your plan book, think about the individual students in the class, their strengths and weaknesses, their interests, running over both their hard grades and your personal knowledge of each of them. You start choosing, rather than creating from scratch. You start choosing, rather than writing as fast as you can and sprinting to the copy machine and praying there won't be a long line because you're already two minutes late to class. Like a good quarterback, you know exactly how you will march your team down the field. You have knowledge about the plays that will work and the plays that might not work. There will be no need for a Hail Mary pass with four seconds on the clock. You will make a series of deliberate choices, moving from the desperate state in which some teachers find themselves to that of measured control.

Imperative 5

Correspond
With Grace,
Tact, and Detail

T eachers write often. We write e-mails to students, parents, and colleagues. We write memos, letters, and agendas; feedback on papers, tests, quizzes, and projects; recommendations for students and colleagues; and speeches for presentations to small or large bodies of students, parents, and teachers.

Whether you like writing or despise it, whether you do it well or poorly, it is increasingly relevant to the work we do in schools. Writing becomes particularly important when it involves information about students or exchanges that seek to support student development. Think about the fallout from an e-mail exchange with a parent wherein you lost your cool and wrote some things you shouldn't have. Think about the time you sent or received a memo with unclear information or wrote a note to a colleague without thinking about what you really wanted to convey.

Your correspondences may have unintended consequences. At worst, they will function like grenades, severing ties and putting individuals at cross-purposes. At best, they will unify constituents around a cause or put people in an empowered, problem-solving position. Ultimately, if it is clear and thoughtful, the writing we do in school will consistently save us time while also extending and clarifying the work we do in our classrooms.

THE FIRST PRINCIPLE OF TEACHER CORRESPONDENCE: BE SUPPORTIVE AND GRACEFUL

Like any effective writing, writing in a school setting calls for an awareness of your audience. To whom are you writing, and what is at stake for him or her? At the same time, you need to be aware of your own position in the conversation as well as any implied connections you have to other facets of the school. For you are never *just a teacher*. You are a member of a department and perhaps a team within a department. You are a member of a school with a certain mission, a school that has made certain commitments to the student and parent body that it serves. If you speak independently of these considerations, you might do damage to a colleague's work, a department's policies, or a school's reputation.

For example, let's say a teacher writes a quick e-mail to a student about a project that she failed to turn in on time (see Correspondence Box 5.1). He's been fed up with her all year, and he feels that this final act of disrespect demands some pointed language. He writes quickly and does not have any time to reread his message. He hits send.

Correspondence Box 5.1

| To: |
| Cc: |
| Subject: |

Sue:

Your project on "The Physics of the Everyday World" was due YESTERDAY!!! You have been very irresponsible, as has been your pattern all semester. If I don't have the project in my hands—not sent via e-mail or put on my desk or some other place where it "might get lost"—you will receive a zero. I'm done making concessions for you, chasing you around the building, dealing with excuses from your parents, nurses, and anyone else who will vouch for you. The next move is yours.

From the point of view of a teacher, this honestly worded e-mail might seem justified, and it certainly serves a purpose. The student clearly has a history of missing deadlines, and it sounds like she frequently calls on the adults in her life to bail her out. The teacher is also clearly frustrated and trying to resolve the situation by establishing a clear consequence. But from the point of view of a department chair, administrator, parent, or student, this e-mail might be less effective at attaining the kind of results that are good for the student, the teacher, and the school.

Other Lenses

A department chair will read the e-mail to Sue with an eye on department or school policy. In particular, the chair will focus on the teacher's penalty: "If I don't have the project in my hands—not sent via e-mail or put on my desk or in some other place where it 'might get lost'—you will receive a zero." Is this consistent with what other department members would do in the same situation? Is this consistent with what is expected from teachers throughout the school? Unless the answers are yes and yes, this part of the e-mail has a chance of doing more harm than good. The teacher wants (or should want) the project and not a series of meetings wherein he has to explain why he has altered policy to add an extra strict penalty for a piece of late work. He wants (or should want) to discuss physics skills and personal habits with the student, not policy with an administrator or a parent.

From the point of view of an administrator, whose job is to make sure the school is following a student-centered and supportive mission, this e-mail might be even more problematic. The all-caps YESTERDAY and the three exclamation points at the end of the first sentence are a sign of anger, which is not an acceptable emotion in a school setting. The teacher also has announced, publicly, that he is "done" with the student, which is also unacceptable. Absent from the e-mail is a motivating or coaching tone, which is vital to student achievement. The bottom line is that this teacher has said a lot, implied a lot more, and let fly with a year's worth of frustration. To support the teacher, the administrator will have to ask for documentation of the problems leading up to this outburst, costing the teacher time. To reprimand the teacher, the administrator also will need to use up part of the teacher's time that can surely be better spent.

Meanwhile, the student and the student's parent might read this e-mail and go on the defensive or offensive. They might be wondering about the lack of an incentive. If the student doesn't turn in the project, she will not receive credit. But what if she does turn it in? The e-mail doesn't say anything about completion. Will she receive a D? They might see this e-mail as a teacher cutting a tie, and they might even talk to other members of the community about this teacher's behavior. These responses serve to change the condition of the student-teacher relationship and turn attention away from what is most important: that the student accept responsibility for her work and complete the work in a timely fashion.

Returning to the Teacher's Point of View

Clearly, when a student is consistently irresponsible, this must be addressed. But I believe patience is a precondition of all teacher-student relationships. If students were perfectly responsible, perfectly respectful, perfectly skilled, teachers would all be out of a job. While I do not believe that teachers should kowtow to administrators or parents, I am suggesting that with every correspondence, large or small, teachers can, intentionally or unintentionally, do harm or good to their school's mission. If you sit down to write an e-mail to a parent or student, or anyone challenging what you do, ask yourself if you have a right, as a paid professional, to allow your emotions to cloud your primary task—that is, to help students reach their potential more quickly than they would without you. Also ask yourself if you have the time to deal with the fallout from a poorly worded e-mail. And finally, ask yourself if you have the political capital to potentially damage your reputation. You can be firm without causing resentment. You can uphold standards without sending a message that a student is somehow a bad person because he or she did not meet the standard.

This example points to the first principle of successful writing in schools, elaborated here:

Principle 1

Your professional correspondence should focus on an unbiased presentation of information, especially when it is related to student progress. Language fraught with emotion or multiple meanings has the potential to cause emotional reactions or misinterpretations, moving you further from the purpose of the correspondence, which is to help students. To correspond effectively, work to clarify your message (information), convey a supportive tone, and visualize your audience. In short, aspire in all correspondence to the conditions of grace, which encompasses three qualities: elegance, politeness, and generosity.

Keeping this principle in mind, we can rephrase the original e-mail to Sue, conveying a clear point, adding a dollop of motivation, and extending the same helping hand a teacher should offer to any student in his or her care. Correspondence Box 5.2 shows a possible rewrite.

Correspondence Box 5.2

To:
Cc:
Subject:

Dear Sue,

I hope everything is okay. Your project was due yesterday, and I'm a bit concerned that I have not heard from you. Attached to this e-mail is another copy of the project guidelines. I urge you to submit your project as soon as possible, even if you feel that it still needs work. Remember, after I grade the projects, I will give all students a chance to revise their work, but if you lose too many points due to tardiness, you will have a harder time earning the kind of grade of which you are capable. Please contact me if you have any questions.

This e-mail starts on a personal note ("I hope everything is okay"), reminds the student what is owed, reminds her about the guidelines, speaks to her possible anxiety (turn it in even if it is not perfect), and gives her an incentive (a chance to revise). However, this incentive is not limitless; it will only help her if she turns in her work before losing too many points for tardiness. The e-mail ends with a pat on the back and some added support.

Does this perpetually late student deserve such treatment? The answer, it seems to me, doesn't matter. What matters, first and foremost, is that the work comes in and that the student goes through the process of completing the task, internalizing what completion feels and looks like.

THE SECOND PRINCIPLE OF TEACHER CORRESPONDENCE: GET SPECIFIC

The second principle of effective teacher correspondence asks us to focus on the content of our correspondences. In the above e-mail to Sue, the content was never in question. Sue had failed to turn in a project; even when the tone of the e-mail was inflammatory, it clearly addressed the issue of late work. Not all matters that require correspondence will be as easy to articulate.

In particular, I'm thinking about correspondence intended to give students, parents, administrators, or learning specialists an update on student learning. At some schools, this update comes in the form of formal quarterly checklists or comments. In other schools, it happens on a more informal basis, coming only when requested (by someone with a stake in the matter) or necessitated (by a teacher's concern over a student's lack of progress).

Let's move to an example of an English teacher who is asked to give an update on Eric, a student who currently has a B– average. The parents are concerned that Eric is not trying hard enough, and as a result, he is not reaching his potential. The teacher writes the message shown in Correspondence Box 5.3.

Correspondence Box 5.3

> To:
> Cc:
> Subject:
>
> Dear Mr. and Mrs. Smith:
>
> I should begin by saying that I really enjoy working with Eric. He is a polite young man, if a bit on the quiet side. As you know, Eric's current average is an 81%, or B–. His most recent paper on *The Great Gatsby* was a 78%. His thesis demonstrated inconclusive critical thinking, and his textual evidence proved that he did not read the text with precision. Added to this 78% was a series of vocabulary grades (on which Eric earned a B– and a B) and reading quizzes (on which Eric earned a B– and a C). Ultimately, these grades are lower than they should be—as you know, I think Eric is a bright kid. Essentially, he needs to work on his critical thinking skills (as evinced by the paper) and his reading skills (as evinced by the paper and the reading quizzes).

The tone of this e-mail is supportive, so it clearly abides by the first principle related to tone and audience. Also, many parents will be content with such an e-mail; it certainly sounds like it means something.

In reality, though, the contents of the e-mail could mean dozens of things. How are critical thinking skills related to the development of a thesis? Does this mean that the student needs to include more textual evidence, stronger analysis of the textual evidence, or argumentative topic sentences? Perhaps more important, does he annotate properly? What might be a solution for each of these items? How might a student check to make sure he or she is actually improving in each of these areas?

Unfortunately, parents do not always know how to ask the right questions, or they do not feel comfortable asking a teacher (especially a writing teacher!) to write more clearly. Essentially, what is needed in this example is a follow-up question asking the teacher to unpack his comments and to formulate actionable steps to help Eric slowly and systematically improve his critical thinking and reading.

Parents may respond to e-mails such as the one presented above in a variety of ways. Some typical parent responses are listed below. We can hone in on the problem with the original e-mail if we examine what these responses might do (or not do) for the student in question.

- The parents will accept the remarks and turn their attention to the student, asking him to try harder. But how will a 15-year-old boy with a possible motivation issue find the maturity and foresight to both plan and implement a plan to improve his critical thinking and reading skills? What's the first step? The second step? How will he know if he is proceeding in the right direction?
- The parents will look at the grades and decide that they want to help the student raise them. As a long-term spur to learning, the question "how can you raise your grade?" is the wrong one. Yes, grades are important. But a student with a critical thinking or reading issue requires ongoing formative assessment. An improved grade on an assessment may not mean that he is acquiring the necessary skills for his future education and life. It might just mean that he figured out how to take his teacher's test or that he memorized the answers to the test.

Effective educators are trained professionals, and they should act the part, identifying student strengths and weaknesses as well as helping students to grow academically, socially, and emotionally. The second principle of teacher correspondence can be stated thus:

Principle 2

In a conversation with a parent, teachers have a responsibility to be specific. They have a responsibility to have the kinds of conversations that lead to accountability (on all fronts) and growth.

The e-mail to Eric's parents could therefore be rewritten as in Correspondence Box 5.4 (additions are in bold).

Correspondence Box 5.4

To:
Cc:
Subject:

Dear Mr. and Mrs. Smith:

I should begin by saying that I really enjoy working with Eric. He is a polite young man, if a bit on the quiet side. As you know, Eric's current average is an 81%, or B−. His most recent paper on *The Great Gatsby* was a 78%. His thesis demonstrated inconclusive critical thinking. **Although I use these terms frequently in class, let me elaborate. Eric started with an idea about the "death of the American dream," but he did not prove that idea through a series of argumentative body paragraphs. One look at his topic sentences shows that he veered drastically from his intended argument. If he chooses to rewrite the paper, under my attention I hope, he should start by reformulating his topic sentences, making sure that they provide clear steps for his argument. This would also be a great time for us to go over his annotations. I'm wondering if he is taking notes while he is reading. Given his recent scores on reading quizzes (a B− and a C), I also wonder if Eric understands how to derive meaning from words when they are placed in literary contexts. As you know, words mean different things when they are placed in different contexts; like many students his age, Eric is still learning how to work through complicated passages in our nightly reading. Feel free to read with him from time to time, and talk about your reactions. At this critical stage in his development, Eric needs partners in his learning—at school and at home.**

This e-mail represents a way of thinking about students that is prompted by a habit of specificity. Sure, it takes a bit longer to write than a regular e-mail that falls back on the old, familiar terminology. But an e-mail like this serves as a blueprint for a student's success. A parent can refer to it and use it to create goals for his or her child. A teacher or tutor working with the child can print it out and use it as a checklist of things to work on (topic sentences, annotations, vocabulary in context).

As teachers, we are always accountable for student learning, whether we are standing in front of a class or composing an e-mail. What's more, we can make the most of the time we have by using e-mail to close as many gaps as possible. The e-mail above has the potential to lead to a student-teacher meeting and a parent-student meeting. It establishes clear parameters for these meetings, too.

Getting Specific

I've had conversations with teachers wherein I've raised the idea of specificity, and they often respond negatively. They don't feel that specificity is always possible. The learning process is, they think, a messy, at times irrational, affair. I agree, but I also think that a teacher has to be able to cut through the messiness and the irrationality to create a clear starting point for learning. Like the doctor who might not know exactly what is wrong, the teacher can learn a lot even from a failed treatment of a misnamed problem.

To become more adept at specificity, teachers can implement a variety of strategies.

1. Keep a journal like the one mentioned in Chapter 4. After class, on a rotating basis, write about the achievements and stumbling blocks of a few students. Throughout the year, this will give you an evolving picture of the learners you deal with on a daily basis. Also, when asked or moved to comment on a student, you will have a ready source of specific material.

2. When you write about students, have some of their work in front of you. Quote from it to demonstrate what works and what does not work. You also can quote from your own comments on the student work, especially if they are prescriptive in nature.

3. When you write about students, include or quote from a rubric.

4. Send home examples of a few different successful versions of the assignment.

5. When you write about students, avoid empty adjectives and false praise.

Specificity concerning students is a habit just as much as using muddy, jargon-heavy writing is a habit. It starts with the way you structure an assignment, articulate learning targets, give feedback to students, and ultimately create reports about the progress of students.

CORRESPONDING WITH COLLEAGUES

Teachers don't simply write to students or parents. They also write to each other—a lot. They write e-mails about everything from an upcoming meeting to requests for coverage. They write memos about upcoming events.

Not surprisingly, attention to tone and specificity, as mentioned above, should guide all teacher-to-teacher correspondence as well.

If you send an e-mail with the wrong tone to a student, you will affect one student's learning process. If you send an e-mail with the wrong tone to a colleague, you will weaken the foundation of collegiality required to support all students' learning processes. So while it might be satisfying to write a nasty e-mail to a colleague every once in a while, here are some reasons to refrain from using a tone you might regret.

- Your e-mail can be saved and forwarded. Do you really want to create a piece of lasting evidence that shows you being rude to a colleague?
- It might lead to an ugly reply, escalating a situation to the point where it will require resolution (time) or perhaps never be resolved.
- You might sever a working relationship that will need to be leveraged in the future to support a student or a program.
- Even if everything returns to normal, the receiver of the message will probably never forget it.

And here are some guidelines for your correspondence with colleagues:

- Don't send an e-mail to explain your feelings, especially if you are angry. Instead, use e-mail to set up a meeting to discuss a particular topic, especially if it is bothering you.
- Don't use the Cc: function as a power play.
- Don't Bcc: unless you are willing to deal with someone finding out about it.
- If you really feel the need to write an emotional or angry e-mail, save it as a draft or send it to yourself and reread it in a day or two. Then decide.
- Do keep your e-mails short and focused.

The last point about brevity is worth discussing further. Keeping it in mind will help you to send lean, specific e-mails on which teachers can rely as they move throughout their busy days. Good or bad, e-mail is truly a catchall for many teachers, serving as a calendar, information warehouse, and repository of personal reminders. When you send an e-mail, realize that, although they may only skim it the first time they read it, your colleagues will often return to it right before it is needed. All around my school, I routinely hear the following exchanges.

"Where is that meeting?"

"I don't know. Check the e-mail. It was sent a few days ago."

Or,

"What did we decide to do for the final exam?"

"Check the notes. The team leader sent an e-mail after our department meeting."

When you sit down to write an e-mail (or any other form of electronic correspondence), make sure every word serves a purpose—and start writing well when you write in the subject line.

By writing clear subject lines in e-mails, you help people do their jobs on the go, which is the primary way most teachers function. The following subject lines, regarding an agenda for an upcoming meeting, are listed in order of least effective to most effective.

Hola

No Subject

Meeting

Meeting Thursday

Meeting Thursday, May 9, Room 20

Agenda for Thursday Meeting (May 9, Room 20)

Although you don't want your subject lines to run too long, you do want them to serve as clear anchors of specific content that people can quickly spot and use.

WHEN TO STOP WRITING

Correspondence has a limit. If things are becoming tangled; if the conversation is beginning to be built upon interpretation instead of information and action; if too many adults are being implicated, creating a layer of flab around the central concern (the student); if a parent is inadvertently trying to shield the student from an important learning experience; if emotion is clouding the water . . . pick up the phone, or set up a face-to-face meeting.

Imperative 6

Process or Drown

After the birth of our son, my wife and I acquired all kinds of devices to capture the precious images of his "firsts." His first words, his first steps, his first slice of pizza: between the digital camera, the cell phone camera, and the digital video recorder, we've got them all. Additionally, we have thousands of other images as well. Like many people we know, my wife and I do a great job of collecting snapshots and video, but we're fairly lousy in the editing department.

I don't think this is necessarily a modern problem, resulting from the ease of storing photographs digitally. My mother still has boxes of photos from my childhood, and she has been saying for years that she will organize them, and my father, who favors his old Polaroid, has acquired stacks and stacks of prints without any recognizable pattern or order.

So what's going on with my family? Are we simply lazy? Not particularly. Are we unwilling to look through our family photographs? Not the last time I checked.

I think there's something much more fundamental, much more human at work. It's the same problem that strikes newly married couples when they try to pick out 42 (of 742) pictures for their wedding album, the same problem that faces a documentary filmmaker who sits down with 50 hours of raw footage, the same problem that faces an author who sits down with a bloated manuscript . . .

And it's the same problem that faces teachers everywhere when they sit down with (or run from) their piles of papers, notes, handouts, computer files, websites, videos, parent requests, and e-mails. There's an agony in selecting from the multitude of possible details that accrue in our photo collections, our home movies, our writing, and our teaching.

There's an agony in selecting, but a danger in failing to select, especially for teachers.

If we never shape the information for which we alone are responsible, we will never isolate the story of the school year and its various characters. We will never know the extent to which students have improved, never follow through on the small things that make good teachers great teachers and good schools great schools, never keep track of the fine work we have done in the classroom. We will never learn as much as we could learn from the things that did not go well. Instead, metaphorically, we simply will fall into the waves of information that wash over us, hold our breaths, and hope to be washed ashore at the start of summer.

Taking charge of what I call the period after last period (PALP) can help. During this block of time, the 20 or 30 minutes after your last teaching responsibility of the day, you can fashion the absolutely critical habit of processing your work. You can learn to effectively end the day or the week in order to make sure that the right story is taking shape.

When I talk about processing, I purposefully conflate the terms processing and story. When we think of processing, we usually think of mechanical actions, of computers. But when we think of stories, we think of beginnings, middles, and endings; we think of sense, of meaning, of humanity. If you can think of processing as story shaping, you will not simply think of it as an empty activity or as paper pushing. It will become a viable and honorable part of your day. For if you process well, you work meaningfully, and in turn, your work makes meaning.

This chapter, then, is an example of how we might approach the PALP and use it to affect positive change in our school communities. It turns out, there are almost as many ways to process as there are things to process.

PROCESSING PROCESSING: A PERFORMANCE PIECE

Before I started writing this book, I defined processing as "taking anything that is already created (i.e., a message, a database) and making sense of it." Apparently, my early, working definition was quite limited. According to the Encarta World English Dictionary that comes bundled with my Microsoft Word program, the verb form of the word *process* has almost a dozen different definitions. Most are worth thinking about in terms of the knowledge work that educators complete on a daily basis. They all shed a different light on a fundamental task.

To process means

1. **"To treat or prepare something in a series of steps or actions, for example, using chemicals or industrial machinery"**

   In "The Heroic Checklist," (*Fast Company*, March 2008), the Brothers Heath, mentioned earlier for their work in *Made to Stick*, praise the lowly checklist as a decidedly useful tool, even in the biggest and most important businesses on the planet. They champion checklists because they "can educate people about the best course of action" and "can help people avoid blind spots in complex environments" (p. 66).

In the complex environment of schools, checklists can provide needed clarity and stability. And, perhaps more important, they can help you turn your attention to higher order thinking, to creative endeavors, to student needs. Additionally, they are especially helpful at the end of a long day, when you might be apt to overlook details.

Therefore, every now and then, use the PALP to produce and use checklists. Ask yourself, what activities do you end up doing over and over again? Would a checklist help you? Would a checklist help your students or colleagues? Examples of useful checklists include

- A checklist for students to use when they start a class period
- A checklist for students to use when they end a class period and prepare for their homework assignment
- A checklist of the top 10 major writing principles
- A checklist of how to read a textbook
- A checklist for the coffee maker in the faculty room that always overflows because some people do not know how to use it
- A checklist that will help you prepare for back-to-school night

Clearly, these checklists may not be perfect the first time you create and use them, but you can always add to them as you go along, building a master repository to help you quickly move through certain procedures that creep up time and time again, year after year.

2. **"To treat light-sensitive film or paper with chemicals in order to make a latent image visible"**

Applying this definition to our teaching lives, plain and simple, urges us to make meaning, to make sense. I am reminded of a time early last spring when I decided to dive into a pile of papers that had been stagnating in a corner of my desk. I knew that there was nothing time sensitive in the pile, but each day it wore on my nerves because I knew it contained value.

When I finally went through it, I recycled about one-fourth of the pile, filed most of the rest, and discovered a short reflection piece from a student with whom I was having trouble connecting. As soon as I saw the piece, I remembered that I had set it aside with the intention to follow up on it. It contained a few small details about the life of the student, and I was convinced that the details (regarding an interest in music) would give me the "in" I would need to forge a bond with this young man. This approach worked almost instantly, almost as if he were waiting for me to approach him and talk to him about his musical interests. When I got to know him, I was able to motivate him to try a few new things in my class and to put more time into his work. Although he couldn't articulate this principle, he clearly wanted me to approach him first as a human being, then as a student.

I literally pulled this relationship out of one of the trays I use for miscellaneous papers . . . papers that, in the rush of a school day, I had simply pushed aside, unable or unwilling to commit to (1) their disposal or (2) the actions they would suggest. I would have missed a great opportunity if I didn't take the time to comb through the papers and bring the latent image it contained (in this case, a strengthened relationship) to the surface. You might be sitting on the same kind of powerful information—and not even know it. A note to call a parent and share some good news, an article that might contain just the insight you need, test data that might inform a future lesson. Although these details in themselves might not be monumental cornerstones of your career, finding the time, energy, and focus to tend to them and others like them very well might shape your entire career.

3. **"To deal with somebody or something according to an established procedure"**

Procedures in schools can be harmful if you use them to replace thinking or to eliminate the possibility of compassion, flexibility, or kindness. However, you also can rely on procedure to process students and make sure they are getting what they need from your class or your program. Certain things should be standard operating procedure. Students who perform below a certain level, whatever that level is determined to be, should be called in for extra help. Students who exhibit certain behavior patterns should be counseled or at least engaged in conversations with trusted adults. These procedures, even if they are rigid, are built on a foundation of concern for students.

A good PALP session, focused strictly on corralling your students and raising your awareness of any outliers, can lead to potential intervention for some. But if you never take the time to step back and examine student behaviors and results, you might miss the very signs that should be calling you to action. Remember, the brain becomes less attentive to patterns that it experiences on a regular basis. You cannot allow yourself to become numb to the patterns, especially the dangerous patterns, that emerge in your classrooms.

4. **"To chop, mix, or otherwise prepare food in a food processor or blender"**

Due to our time constraints at school, we tend to accept things as they are and simply trudge through them. We might complain about certain classes, certain technological malfunctions, certain meetings, certain colleagues, but we rarely take those few steps back, those perspective-gathering steps, to modify the systems that guide our work.

Processing, in the food processing sense, reminds us to stir things (radically) on occasion. Perhaps a team or committee is growing stagnant and failing to fulfill its duty. Would it help to add a few new voices? Perhaps one of your classes seems listless, in a rut. Would it help to change a few posters in the room, to ask the class to help you decorate a section of the room, to change the configuration of the classroom? Perhaps you are just not feeling invigorated at school. Would it help to eat lunch with a new group of people or form a study group with some teachers from other schools?

5. **"To use a computer program to work on data in some way, for example, to sort a database or recalculate a spreadsheet"**

Examining data is a great way to orient yourself in the midst of a busy semester. It can tell you if students are meeting your learning targets, if you need to try a different strategy, and if you are moving at an appropriate pace to accomplish your objectives. It can tell you if your students are doing better than last year's students and if they have, in fact, made strides over where they were last year.

I know that not all teachers are comfortable with data. Some have little or no training in Excel, little or no training in statistics. Some fear that data imply an accountability factor. While that may be true, I am talking here primarily about teacher-driven data initiatives that originate on the local, classroom level. Although teachers may choose to share these data with colleagues, the data's sole purpose, *as I discuss it here,* is to help teachers quickly spot trends and patterns that might be useful to them as they continue, and finish, their classroom instruction for the year.

One of the opening insights from Theodore Creighton's (2007) highly accessible book, *Schools and Data*, helps to create a meaningful distinction. He writes that, "Data analysis does not have to involve complex statistics. Data analysis in schools involves (1) collecting data and (2) using available data for the purpose of improving teaching and learning" (p. 2–3). When I talk about using data, midweek, in the middle of a busy semester, I am not talking about collecting data. I am talking about using the data you have already collected: the data that fill up your grade book, your inbox, your notebooks, and your student folders.

Many teachers might wonder where to start when they sit down during a PALP with the intention of examining existing data. To help you get started, and guide you through the process, consider the following:

- You can review attendance patterns and grades. Is there a correlation that you can notice and report to individual students or parents?
- You can review a certain type of assessment that you give on a regular basis. For example, are the grades on your vocabulary quizzes going up across the board? Are the grades on your reading quizzes going up? Are some students failing to improve as much as the rest of the students? What can you do to help these students?
- If you use a system like Moodle or Blackboard, where you can examine the last time each student logged into the system, you can review the level of engagement of each student and compare that to his or her overall grade. Again, this might give you information to share with a student or parent. If students are not logging in to the class homepage, chances are they are getting their information from other students, which might or might not give them a clear picture of what they need to do to thrive in your class.

6. "To straighten curly hair using lye"

At first, this definition seems completely out of character with our school lives. Using lye on curly hair? The connotation is archaic at best. But we all have curly, tangled spots in our professional lives, and they usually involve someone else, a personality conflict, or a relationship wherein the communication is not as clear and direct as it could be. Perhaps the hardest form of processing to use, this definition asks us to identify and enter these knotty, interpersonal patches and figure out how to make them workable.

Susan Scott's (2004) book, *Fierce Conversations: Achieving Success at Work and in Life, One Conversation at a Time*, is the definitive primer on how to process your working life in this way. Although she would argue that you cannot, and should not, straighten the curly aspects of reality, she grounds her work in a fundamental belief that there are conversations that we are not having that we should be having and that might affect meaningful change in our working lives (p. 20).

So you might use a PALP to make a list of conversations that you should have and then set up times to follow through on those resolves. You might need to clear the air with a particular student, with a parent, or with a colleague. You might need to bring something to your principal's attention. You may have witnessed an inappropriate interaction between a colleague and a student or between two colleagues and feel the need to intervene— or at least call attention to the fact that the exchange made you uncomfortable.

These conversations are certainly not easy, and they can go wrong. But they also allow you to improve your school climate through an honest presentation of your feelings and your observations. (Note: if you have trouble even conceiving of entering these kinds of discussions, spend some PALP time reading Scott's book.)

7. **"To discuss the interpersonal dynamics and emotional content of an event or situation"**

When we move too quickly or when we have too many things on which to keep tabs, it is easy to forget about the emotions in the rooms we inhabit. We just want to get in, make sure we do our jobs, and get out.

But the literature related to emotion and leadership, empathy and leadership, and the importance of social and emotional intelligence in the functioning of organizations, has made (and continues to make) a strong case that we each have a responsibility to tend to the emotional climates in our classrooms, meeting rooms, and schools.

Think about the teams or groups you lead. Does everyone seem happy? Who can you ask to find out for sure? Is it worth doing a quick climate survey, focusing on people's comfort level, asking people if they feel like they are making a contribution that matters? Are your presentations to groups geared toward different learning styles? As Bennis and Biederman (1997) write, "Great groups are organizations fully engaged in the thrilling process of discovery" (p. 7). Have you checked lately to see if your groups are fully engaged and fully focused?

Taking It Seriously

By taking seriously and engaging in the various types of processing, we can tend to so many different aspects of school life, such as the important, though mundane, operational details that keep things moving on a daily basis; the students who have coasted past us, below the radar; the habit that is holding us back from reaching our full potential; the data that can help us to see the effect we are having at a time when we can still make changes; and the conversations that we need to have in order to mend or extend certain key relationships. Figure 6.1 offers a snapshot of how you might use the PALP to process your school days and in turn work more meaningfully, more deliberately.

This section poses a difficult challenge in what, I hope, is a manageable daily dose. It urges you to step out of your normal workflow, no matter how urgent it seems, to think about larger concerns—for about 20 or 30 minutes each day.

If you are having trouble grasping this as a workable concept, I ask you to think about *impact*. Do you want to have a small impact tomorrow or a large impact six months from now? Do you want to forge a career the best outcomes of which result from chance and the worst outcomes of which result from preventable accidents, or do you want a career of deliberate decisions and planned excellence? By starting with small doses of processing, you will build habits that will sustain and inform your work throughout your career.

We often get stuck doing the thing that absolutely needs to be done. That's fine. That's part of being a functional professional. But if we never take the time to think about the results of our work, the patterns that are emerging, how we are working, and if we are working the right way, we might be missing the biggest gains available to us and, in turn, to our students.

Figure 6.1	
Definition	*Application*
1. "To treat or prepare something in a series of steps or actions, for example, using chemicals or industrial machinery"	Look over the broad range of activities you complete on a daily, weekly, monthly, or yearly basis. Do patterns emerge? Do you find yourself reinventing the wheel? Write some checklists or develop some procedures.
2. "To treat light-sensitive film or paper with chemicals in order to make a latent image visible"	Are any stories being lost in the daily grind? How can you rescue them, shape them, and finish them? How can you publicize them?
3. "To deal with somebody or something according to an established procedure"	Think about your students. Do any of them need to be reined in or pulled in? Examine your class lists, your class notes, your grades, and your hunches. Do any of your students require intervention, whether academic or personal?
4. "To chop, mix, or otherwise prepare food in a food processor or blender"	Is anything stale or stagnant in your teaching life? What can you cut or shuffle or rotate? What will put you in a new situation with new students or colleagues?
5. "To use a computer program to work on data in some way, for example, to sort a database or recalculate a spreadsheet"	What data have you already collected, and what can you do with them? How can these data inform your decision making? On the other hand, what data-related questions do you have? What data do you need to answer the questions? Where can you find the data?
6. "To straighten curly hair using lye"	Susan Scott (2004) says it all: "What is the conversation [you've] been unable to have with senior executives, with [your] colleagues, with [your] direct reports, with [your] customers, with [your] life partner, and most important, with [yourself], with [your] own aspirations, that if [you] were able to have, might make the difference, might change everything?" (20)
7. "To discuss the interpersonal dynamics and emotional content of an event or situation"	Are your teams and classes working as effectively as they might? Are the members of your teams or classes fulfilled and confident that you are the kind of leader who will help them reach their full potential? Do any members of your teams or your classes have bad relationships with other members of the team or class? How can you be sure that these relationships do not pollute the relationships among the other team or class members?

Imperative 7

Become a Radical Learner

A s teachers, day-to-day, we learn what we need to learn. We brush up on a formula or a fact; we learn to e-mail attachments or how to post comments on an electronic message board. These tiny gains keep us moving a step ahead of our students, and they are admirable. But I contend that there is a more transformative kind of professional development available to teachers—and that the kind of growth it makes available is no longer optional.

The quick rate of change in our society may be the only constant we have left. Everything's evolving, from cell phones to fitness, social networks to cars, nutrition, the media, and reading. If you want proof, think about how the following words have impacted, or are beginning to impact, our daily habits: iPhones, Wii, Facebook, hybrids, Whole Foods, blogging, Kindles. Oh, and Google.

I am not concerned with whether or not these entities or devices survive. I list them to make you aware of the proliferation of innovation and change in our culture. In a time when everything is uncertain, when everything is changing, when tomorrow won't necessarily look or feel like today, only one thing is certain: Learning is not optional, and learning is never finished. We have to get comfortable with being slightly uncomfortable, with being in a state of constant transition, with living with Version 2.0 while simultaneously looking forward to Versions 2.1 and 2.2 and 2.3, ad infinitum.

To access this state of continual growth, we need to throw ourselves full force into the learning process, rife as it is *and must be* with setbacks and digressions. We have to approach our professional lives the way personal trainers approach our bodies.

Trainers say that you will not substantially increase your fitness level if you do the same round of exercises everyday. Your body learns to cope with the habitual exertion. I believe that we can fall into similar ruts in our teaching careers, conducting our business in ways that are most comfortable to us and, therefore, diminish our long-term potential as educators. Allow me to make some rather grand suggestions about how you might grow as a teaching professional.

You could plant a garden or climb a mountain. If you're a math or science teacher, you could spend the summer reading the classics. If you're an English or history teacher, you could take a lab science course at a local college. You could interview a lawyer or a project manager or spend the day with an architect or an artist. You could, but you probably won't because you just don't have time to spend on "extraneous" activities, things that don't produce immediate results, or quick fixes. You just don't have the time to spend on your own growth. What a huge loss for our schools.

On the surface, my suggestions have nothing to do with backward design, differentiated instruction, assessment, or any other skill set with which teachers are supposed to be comfortable. And they seem to have nothing to do with what actually happens in the classroom. But peer a little bit deeper.

Let's say you decide to plant a garden. You are forced to start at the end, figuring out what you want your garden to yield. Do you want tomatoes and zucchini? Do you want herbs? What kinds of herbs? As you answer these questions, you develop a plan to ensure that your results are in line with your expectations. Along the way, you are forced to look closely at the effects of your actions and the weather conditions, make necessary modifications, and guide the plants toward your projected outcome for them. The vegetables or spices that land on your table are the direct product of some of the major principles of backward design and assessment. Growing them has given you the chance to practice a fundamental skill set in a completely new context.

But what if you're the English teacher who takes my advice to spend the summer in a science lab? Surely that won't be productive. Surely your time would be better spent reading some of the classics you missed along the way. Then again, your time in the lab might be the best thing you can do for the one student you might understand the least—that is, the one student who understands you the least. What does class feel like for a student who "just doesn't get it" or who has to struggle to catch up or who forgot, or never learned, the necessary background information to thrive in a course? Your time in the lab might provide the perfect empathetic bridge to help you connect with the students who might need you most.

The following reflections and suggestions expand on the notion that enhanced professional development is possible through an enhanced engagement with your professional and personal capacities. They are meant to shake you from your routines and open the possibility for the kind of growth that doesn't just sustain a school year, but a school career. They are also meant to break the rhythm of a book that, until this point, has been designed to fit into your teaching day, to inspire small, non-invasive changes. This chapter is designed to be a bit more invasive, a bit more provocative.

MENTORS AND COLLABORATION

During my first two years as a teacher, I was lucky enough to share a school-apportioned house with Gray Smith, a master teacher from Baltimore. Given that we taught mostly the same classes, we soon developed a routine wherein we would sit at a big table in the study and talk through our daily lesson plans. Although this only took about as long as it would take to watch a sitcom, we covered a lot of ground. We discussed how the previous lesson went and how the next lesson should go. Using a simple question—*Why?*—Gray pushed me to craft my ideas into workable, real-world teaching concepts. Along the way, we talked about pacing, behavior, how to use the board, how to project one's voice, and how to stay organized: the nuts and bolts of teaching.

Then Tucker Curtis came into our lives. Tucker had been teaching for longer than both Gray and me combined, and he loved teaching more than anyone I had known or have known since. Almost immediately, Tucker, Gray, and I started a regular Wednesday-night dinner meeting to talk about teaching. We mostly stayed away from the nuts and bolts items, focusing instead on broad philosophical issues (i.e., What is the role of technology in education? What do students really need to learn in order to prepare for their future? Are the schools we have now the schools we really need?). To stay somewhat focused, we usually grounded our conversations in a common text by someone like Neal Postman or Robert Coles. We had just one rule: we could not talk about anything that happened in school unless we were using the event as an example to elucidate one of the points in the conversation. We avoided gossip fervently, and in fact, when other teachers started joining us, wanting to gab about colleagues or students or parents, we changed our venue.

I know what you're thinking: the scenarios depicted above are once-in-a-lifetime occurrences, and that three educators will rarely have the time and inclination to engage in the kinds of professional conversations that I have described, especially while school is in session! And I'll be the first to admit that I was tremendously lucky. Clearly, I learned and refined a valuable skill set and benefitted from some broad philosophical discourse. At the same time, I gained valuable insights on professional growth, my own and others', that can be applied to all teaching conversation.

My time working alongside Gray Smith taught me that

- *Collaboration should include a reflective element.* Gray and I didn't just share ideas; we discussed the ideas after we tried them, tracking their progress in the real world. We discussed the way their reception was influenced by classroom dynamics, individual student's learning styles, and the differences between classes of kids. This continual monitoring influenced our future planning, keeping our lessons close to the actual students we were teaching, and our collaboration both focused and relevant.

- *Simple, direct questions can lead to terrific conversations about teaching.* In my first few months of teaching, I was helped immeasurably by Gray's favorite questions: How did the lesson go? What worked? What didn't? How do you know? Is there anything that you didn't do that you wanted to do? Did anything surprise you about the way the lesson unfolded? Why? By the end of the year, I was asking him the same kinds of questions. We understood how to hold each other accountable; we understood the value of listening and taking seriously the ideas of our colleagues.

When we joined Tucker, we stretched our wings a bit, worrying less about the particulars of our classrooms and more about our fundamental underpinnings as teachers. This relationship, too, has proven to be continuously instructive, many years later. From it, I learned that

- *You can affect change in your school by altering the typical communication and collaboration patterns.* When talking with colleagues, it's easy to slip into a running commentary about other colleagues, parents, or kids. While this can serve an important "venting" function, it will not help you to solve any of your school's problems. Tucker, Gray, and I would read as much as we could from a selected book during the week; then, when we met, we would sit down and talk about the book, its ideas, what seemed wise or unwise, practical or impractical, possible or impossible. We focused on pure education, the calling of educators, and how teaching might best transform the lives of young people. By focusing on the work of teaching and the larger educational debates affecting our school, we developed our points of view, our ability to see the larger picture, and our pedagogical fluency. This kind of thinking inevitably spilled over into the conversations, meetings, and teaching in which we engaged when we were within the school's walls.

- *Developing your perspective on important topics in education is an invaluable asset that is often lost in the daily scramble of school life.* Being that life on the frontlines of teaching is filled with improvisation, interaction, and unplanned interruptions, it rarely gives teachers a chance to gain perspective on their teaching habits and patterns. By engaging in debates about larger issues in education, you will invariably be forced to rethink the way you operate on the ground level. Reading and discussing Dan Pink's (2005) *A Whole New Mind*, for instance, will challenge you to think about how you design space in your classroom. Reading and discussing the literature on differentiation might make you rethink how you organize desks in your classroom. Studying and discussing diversity in schools might make you rethink the texts you teach, the posters you hang on your walls, and the analogies you use to present concepts.

- *When you have the chance to learn from someone, be the best student you can be—be open, curious, tenacious, and joyful.* All teachers face the dangerous possibility of thinking of themselves as only teachers, only founts of wisdom, only givers of information, and—*retch*—the most interesting person in the classroom. Occasionally slipping into the role of the student is a great opportunity to practice the humility that makes great teachers even better.

RETREATS

Although the "let's grab a cup of coffee and talk about teaching" approach described above should be quite simple, your school's culture might work against it. If everyone perceives himself or herself to be too busy, it is unlikely that you will be able to gather informally on a regular basis to give each other the kind of support I have described. In this case, you can derive some of the same benefits from scheduling a formal retreat with a specific group from your school (for example, a department, the team leaders, or curricular coordinators). The retreat should be held off campus, and it should have a clear agenda. The simplest template I can provide comes from David Allen's (2001) book, *Getting Things Done*. When he talks about priorities, he presents a six-level scale based on an aerospace analogy:

- 50,000+ feet: Life
- 40,000 feet: Three- to five-year goals

- 30,000 feet: One- to two-year goals
- 20,000 feet: Areas of responsibility
- 10,000 feet: Current projects
- Runway: Current actions (pp. 51–53)

A good retreat will give people the time and space to solve immediate problems, to set goals for future projects, to reflect on and recommend changes to the systems that might have contributed to the problems in the first place, to establish priorities for future actions, and to reflect on their long-term visions for their careers and how those careers fit into their lives. Throughout the retreat, the facilitator also should focus on giving people the necessary tools to manage each priority level. For example, if the retreat members need to figure out a way to enact broad curricular change, the facilitator should provide them with some up-to-date literature on leading change, barriers to change, and the psychological implications of change.

Popping the Bubble

I've been talking exclusively about getting together with people from your own school, but this, too, can be a habit that needs breaking. Pop the bubble, jump the fence, shatter the fishbowl: whatever you call it and whatever you do, get out of your school from time to time and find out what's happening in other schools, with other teachers, and with other students.

All groups have their own assumptions, their own roles, their own definitions of the acceptable and the unacceptable. At best, group shorthand allows schools, and teams within schools, to make steady, quick progress. At worst, though, this shorthand breeds complacency, groupthink, and politicking.

When a school thinks it has cornered the market on excellence or loses the ability to judge its own progress or systems, when meetings in schools are filled with silent people who do not agree with the perceived majority, or when more time is spent thinking about who will be in the room during the presentation than the presentation itself, it is possible that a school's shared history is beginning to cloud its judgment.

As a teacher experiencing this kind of stale air in your school, you have two choices: leave and never look back, or acquire some new ideas and introduce them to your school community. If you're interested in the latter, it's time for you to start harnessing the energy that can be derived from other educators at other schools.

MEETING WITH TEACHERS FROM OTHER SCHOOLS

Meeting with teachers in a kind of semiformal workgroup can affirm your practice if you find that you encounter sets of problems similar to those encountered by your colleagues at other schools. Learning that you are not the only teacher dealing with a contingency of unhappy parents or a new emphasis on a standardized test in which you have little faith, for example, can help you to put your own problems in a larger context. At the same time, teachers from other schools might have completely new solutions for your problems, completely new programs that might help your school's mission, or completely different policies that might inform or clarify your own school's decision making.

Getting Started

To develop your list of invitees, consider the purpose of the group. Will it be a group of high school math teachers? A group of teachers interested in curriculum development? A group of teachers who want to share ideas about technology? If you can identify the teachers simply by their job titles, your task is fairly straightforward. Contact all the teachers within a drivable range, and invite them to your first meeting. If you cannot identify teachers simply by looking at their job titles, start with a contact or administrator in the various schools that fall within a drivable range and ask him or her to give you a list of potential teachers who might be interested.

First Meeting

At the first meeting, the agenda should be devoted to laying the groundwork to ensure the perpetuation of the group. If by the end of the first meeting people are not excited and hooked into the group's purpose, chances are they will not return.

After introductions, pass out a generic mission statement, and ask the members to add or subtract as they see fit. This activity will help members feel a sense of ownership over the identity and purpose of the group. A sample mission would read as follows:

> The members of this group will meet several times each year in an effort to learn from each other, share common problems that cut across schools, and propose solutions for dealing with these common problems. They will respect the confidentiality of the group and enter into the conversation with the sole intent of contributing to the growth of each group member.

If you have access to a laptop and a projector, you can project the statement during the discussion and make changes for all to see. Or you can simply take notes as people talk, and circulate a final copy via e-mail.

After discussing the mission statement with the group, ask members to brainstorm a list of problems and topics for the year to come. For example, in a group of English teachers, people might list the following items as problems: how to teach a difficult text in the mixed-ability classroom, how to choose summer reading texts, or how to grade writing assignments. The same group might list the following topics: blogging and the writing process, grammar instruction that matters, booklists, curriculum, reading, and trends shaping the discipline. The purpose of this activity is to set the agenda for upcoming meetings. The problems can provide a warm-up conversation in future meetings; the problems and topics can be assigned to individual group members who will be responsible for (1) finding and e-mailing around a short article that is relevant to the problem or topic and (2) facilitating the discussion at the meeting.

End the first meeting with logistics. Ideally, people will be excited about the group's purpose and dive into a discussion of the logistics out of enthusiasm for the work that the group will do. Project or distribute a blank calendar and set up as many meetings as possible. Decide if the meetings will happen at different schools or at one venue. Figure out a way to pay for or provide refreshments if they are desired.

Subsequent Meetings

If the first meeting goes well, your subsequent meetings should run smoothly. The following rough template provides a clear picture of what you might accomplish.

- Warm-up—Discuss a specific problem, randomly selected from the list generated at the first meeting
- Topic 1—This should be set up in advance, using the list generated at the first meeting
- Topic 2—If time permits (using the list generated at the first meeting)
- Reminders/preparation for next meeting

CONFERENCES AND INSTITUTES

Aside from forming groups inside and outside your home school community, I also suggest that several times in your career you go to an institute or conference where you have the opportunity to live among other educators. In my own career, I have lived at the Center for Talented Youth, the Klingenstein

Summer Institute, and the Exeter Humanities Institute, and I have attended truly well-run conferences like the ETS Assessment Conference with Rick Stiggins. Although these programs and conferences presented me with more than enough work to keep me busy, they also allowed me to take part in some simple, unstructured activities with other educators. During occasional jogs or walks, while preparing or attending meals together or sharing an after-dinner drink, I had the opportunity to learn about schools very different from my own, educators with different priorities or world views, career paths that I had never contemplated, books of which I had never heard, cultural events, and other conferences—in short, many of the things that have shaped me as a person and a professional.

Although it seems like it would be easier to simply stay at home, once you realize how much is happening in the wider world of education, staying home feels a bit less safe, a bit less comfortable.

LISTSERVS, GROUPS, AND SOCIAL NETWORKS

If you simply cannot get away, the Internet is becoming an increasingly bountiful way of connecting with other educators. For more than a decade, listservs and groups have been a terrific way to gather information relevant to both short-term problem solving and long-range planning. For example, Google's Google for Educators Discussion Group not only passes on information about Google's initiatives but also hopes to exist as the "home of a vibrant community of educators" encouraging them to use the space "to start discussions with fellow teachers . . . share ideas about innovation in education; ask questions about where to find teaching resources; [and] tell . . . colleagues about curricula . . . that have worked really well" (para. 1).

Also, social networks, once the province of musicians and the young, are starting to change the game for professional development and collaboration in education. Sites like Classroom 2.0 (http://www.classroom20.com/) and the Independent School Educators Network (http://isenet.ning.com/) are providing models for educators who want to share ideas, lessons, articles, and their professional lives.

Rotation

Here's a quick, relevant story about a bag I use to carry my schoolwork to and from my home each day. One day, this bag started to give off a stale odor. I checked all the usual places, but I couldn't find anything to explain the odor. Busy as usual, I ignored the smell, and after a day or two, I simply got used to it. One day, I accidentally left the bag in another teacher's classroom. When she found it, she put an article she had for me in a side pocket. When I got the bag back, I pulled the papers out of the side pocket and realized, suddenly, the cause of the smell. My two-year-old son had apparently opened the pocket and stashed some Teddy Grahams, tomatoes, and other unrecognizable food in it.

I never used the pocket, so I didn't see it—even when I was looking for the ignoble scent it contained. When investigating the smell, I checked all the usual places, the frequently used places. It took a completely fresh set of eyes, my colleague's, to show me that my bag had other pockets and that one of those other pockets hid a terrible smell. Now that I have cleaned the pocket, I use it. The extra storage space is small but very helpful. It gives me a place to keep my often-lost cell phone and its charger.

In our own careers, we also have pockets that we never open, and these pockets contain the "bad smells" with which we simply learn to live. What's worse, though, is that we also force our students to live with the same negative qualities. If we never change our frame of reference, our way of looking at our own daily practice, we will miss the opportunity to convert our flaws into useful features of our teaching repertoire.

One way to ensure freshness in our teaching lives is to insist on rotation. The first way to create rotation in your school life is to alter something about your job. Teach a different grade or a different elective. Coach a team or serve as a club advisor. Take on an administrative responsibility. The best kind of job rotation will give you access to a segment of the population or a layer of school life with which you are unfamiliar. Contact with the unfamiliar will help you develop new teaching synapses and therefore help you to be more perceptive and empathetic in your dealings with students or colleagues.

For example, let's say you spend a year sitting on a committee that deals with the social and emotional well being of students at your school. On this committee, you learn about the devastating effects of family instability on young students. This is something that you have always known on a commonsense level, but when you actually experience and live through a few cases, you inevitably will develop an entirely new way of looking at your students and understand (or get closer to understanding) why some of them underperform or misbehave.

Other benefits of rotation are articulated by John Gardner (1971) who commented that "Free movement of personnel throughout the organization reduces barriers to internal communication, diminishes hostility between divisions and ensures a freer flow of information and ideas. It contributes on the one hand to versatility of the individual and on the other to fluidity of the organization" (p. 95). These principles play out in almost every possible rotation within a school setting. Moving from teaching to administration allows you to speak to administrators with an understanding of a teacher's perspective. Working closely with administrators gives you a more nuanced view of the decision-making process in schools. Working with student government gives you a chance to understand what bothers students about the way teachers or administrators run the school. Inviting a few students to a faculty technology meeting opens the opportunity for fascinating dialogue, which is bound to affect both the students and the teachers. Coaching or working backstage at a musical shows you sides of your students that you would never see in the classroom. Teaching a higher grade level gives you perspective on what younger students will need to understand in order to thrive at the next level. Teaching at a lower grade level helps you understand the gaps you might need to fill when you work with older students. This final rotation, in turn, also helps to promote dialogue among teachers at all grade levels.

A less radical, although possibly more contested, kind of rotation involves your office space. If you share an office with someone, have you ever thought of switching office mates with someone else?

Over the years, I have shared offices with a number of different people. Although some of the personalities fit better with my working style, I wouldn't change a thing. Without doing any more than simply working and being themselves, my myriad office mates have provided daily learning opportunities for me.

You learn from your office mates when you watch them deal with parents, students, or other colleagues. You learn from your office mates when you observe their approach to relationships. You learn from your office mates when you watch them work. You also learn from your office mates when you turn to them and ask, "What grade would you give this assignment?," or "Do you think I was too harsh or too easy on this student?" You learn from your office mates when you talk to them about workflow, time management, e-mail management, and colleague management. You learn from your office mates when you talk through problems or swap teaching ideas, or when you discuss politics, books, theories, or culture. The list goes on. Should you share an office space, be cognizant of such diverse learning opportunities.

LEADERSHIP

Leadership could have been considered an aspect of rotation, but I think it is important enough to merit its own section. If you want to force yourself to grow, lead something. In school or out, as an administrator, lead teacher, or club leader, leadership will stretch your capacities.

My first act as an official school leader was as the academic dean at the Carlisle site of the Center for Talented Youth. When I arrived for my first day on the job, the site director handed me a clipboard and told me to make sure all the faculty dorm rooms had garbage cans and a working air conditioner. After a few hours of this, I met up with the site director and shared my disbelief with the seemingly meaningless task I had just performed. "I became an academic dean to work with curriculum and teachers," I said. He said, "You wouldn't believe how many teachers develop a bad opinion of the administration based on the fact that their rooms are not set up properly when they arrive. At a boarding program like this, we can't afford to have any friction with the teaching staff. The task you just completed will help you immeasurably when you're trying to have those juicy curriculum discussions that drew you to the job in the first place."

He was right. A few faculty members pulled me aside at the first social function and told me what a good job I was doing, referencing in particular the fact that the previous administration didn't even value them enough to ensure they had garbage cans in their bedrooms.

Everyone who works in schools can benefit from being forced to examine a new layer of school life. My friend and colleague Tony Cuneo, a department chair, has an interesting reason for delegating tasks. He does not delegate solely to move things off his plate. He delegates so that the members of his department can be exposed to the thrill and burden of school leadership. When teachers organize and implement an important change, they feel a strong sense of collegiality and a strong connection to the school. And when they understand how difficult it is to organize meetings, facilitate discussions, build consensus, and ensure follow-through, they learn firsthand about the complexities of school life. This knowledge should curb their own frustrations down the road when new initiatives or policy changes are not moving as quickly or as smoothly as they had hoped. By understanding a small piece of the administrative life, or, more broadly, of school leadership, teachers can become allies in the ever present quest for change in 21st-century schools.

TEACHER AS ARTIST, IMAGINATION AS FUEL

A quick look at the stylistic progression of great artists shows constant growth and reinvention, constant wrong turns that become spectacular innovations. Compare James Joyce's early stories to his final paragraphs in *Ulysses* or *Finnegan's Wake*. Compare John Coltrane's early ballads to his later, radical improvisations. Teaching is at least as much art as it is science, and teachers, like artists, would do well to strive for constant renewal, constant innovation.

Sir Ken Robinson, one of the foremost experts on creativity and potential, had this to say when asked by Susan Bratton (n.d.), "What can we do to change our lives?"

> [If] you want to boil it down in two minutes, it's about two things; it's about habits and habitats. I mean by habit, the routines that we follow during the course of our daily life, the more we do the same thing everyday, the more we think the same way. So, one of the ways of unleashing your creative capacity is to do different things, stimulate your imagination, do things you wouldn't normally do. If you never go to an Opera, go to one. If there are some books you have never read, go and read them. If there are people in your building you have never spoken to, go and speak to them. If you go the same way to work everyday, go some other way. (para. 57)

For teachers, a living spark is vital. Fresh stories or analogies are vital. A willingness to catapult oneself forward on a quest for new knowledge is vital. The wisdom to be open to learning of all kinds is vital. So let me end this chapter where I started it.

Correspondence Box 7.1

To:
Cc:
Subject:

Dear Teacher,

Give yourself permission to plant a garden or climb a mountain. If you're a math or science teacher, spend the summer reading the classics. If you're an English or history teacher, take a lab science course at a local college. Interview a lawyer or a project manager, or spend the day with an architect or an artist. Plan your learning opportunities. Make them deliberately surprising, deliberately unique, and deliberately challenging.

Conclusion

Enjoy Your Balanced Professional Life

keep two quotes pinned to my plan book. The first is by William Least Heat-Moon (1999):

> Had I gone looking for some particular place rather than any place, I'd never have found this spring under the sycamores . . . sitting full in the moment, I practiced on the god-awful difficulty of just paying attention. It's a contention of Heat-Moon's—believing as he does any traveler who misses the journey misses about all he's going to get—that a man becomes his attentions. His observations and curiosity, they make and remake him . . . Whitman calls it "the profound lesson of reception. (p. 17)

The second is by Annie Dillard (1990):

> I have been looking into schedules. Even when we read physics, we inquire of each least particle. What then shall I do this morning? How we spend our days is, of course, how we spend our lives. What we do with this hour, and that one, is what we are doing. A schedule defends from chaos and whim. It is a net for catching days. (p. 31–32)

I refer to these quotes constantly because they present, in their opposition, the inherent contradiction in all teachers' lives: The need to cover material and to develop skills does not always merge perfectly with the serendipitous, digressive quality of a true education. Personally, I have come to value contradiction. If unresolved, its tension can act as an engine for a class, a project, a life. And yet, this lack of resolution need not be chaotic or out of control.

Teachers who thrive in our busy schools know how to create hard edges in their jobs, and these edges give them a place off which to push. They carve out time to address certain tasks, and during that time they remain focused. They don't lose that focus if they have to take a break to attend to the small emergencies that pop up during each and every teaching day. They don't lose their cool when a difficult parent sets up a meeting with them. Instead, they resort to a tried and true method for conflict resolution. They know where certain tasks begin and end; they know when to move on; they know when to revise; they know how to recharge their batteries.

Teachers who thrive in our busy schools call to mind one of Shakespeare's greatest creations: Portia from *The Merchant of Venice*. In some scenes, she is witty. In other scenes, she plays the role of a "perfect" woman. In still other scenes, she goes to court and becomes a tough, smart lawyer. She has the mental fitness and agility to shift shapes depending on the situation and its demands. Clearly, there is a tension between her roles, one that, at times, must pull her in several different directions at once. But in each and every situation she manages to get the job done.

And so . . . it's the week before midterm exams. You're trying to write your exam, but students are coming in for extra help and you have to work though a complicated plagiarism issue with a student, the student's family, and the administration. Alumni are home for winter break, so they're popping in to see you. An administrator has been asking you for some grade information. A parent has demanded to see you. In the midst of this scenario, I have one final suggestion, call it an invitation: Sit back, breathe, and wade into the complexity. If you've read this far, you have plenty of new tools to help you survive and thrive in the schools we have today.

Besides, if you're this busy, perhaps you are doing exactly what you are supposed to be doing. Or more. This is school. This is what you do. This is how you have decided to spend your days.

My friend the poet Kyle Thompson recently sent me a quotation attributed to St. Thomas Aquinas, and I now adapt it for education: *every teacher shares in the dignity of causality*. As you tend carefully to the daily influx of details, your daily interactions with students and colleagues; as you write carefully, grade carefully, plan deliberately; as you contribute meaningfully to the lives of students and others, you lend dignity to the chain of events that drive our flawed and beautiful schools. You lend dignity to the work of student learning, and what could be more important?

References

Allen, D. (2001). *Getting things done: The art of stress-free productivity.* New York: Penguin Books.

Bennis, W., & Biederman, P. W. (1997). *Organizing genius: The secrets of creative collaboration.* New York: Basic Books.

Bratton, S. (n.d.). Sir Ken Robinson: Creativity and innovation expert. In *Personal Life Media* (episode 6). Retrieved December 2, 2008, from http://personallife media.com/podcasts/232-dishymix/episodes/3066-sir-ken-robinson-creativity-and-innovation-expert

Chapman, K. (2007, Winter). Are you working too hard? A conversation with mind/body researcher Herbert Benson, M.D. [Original work published November 2005]. *Harvard Business Review: OnPoint,* 17–21.

Collins, J. (2005). *Good to great and the social sectors: A monograph to accompany* good to great. New York: HarperCollins.

Creighton, T. B. (2007). *Schools and data: The educator's guide for using data to improve decision making.* Thousand Oaks, CA: Corwin Press.

Davies, A. (2007). Involving students in the classroom assessment process. In D. Reeves (Ed.), *Ahead of the curve: The power of assessment to transform teaching and learning* (pp. 59–76). Bloomington, IN: Solution Tree.

Dillard, A. (1990). *The writing life.* New York: Harper Perennial.

Drucker, P. F., & Marciarello, J. A. (2006). *The effective executive in action: A journal for getting the right things done.* New York: HarperCollins.

Frankfurt, H. G. (2005). *On bullshit.* NJ: Princeton University Press.

Gardner, J. W. (1971). *Self renewal: The individual and the innovation society.* New York: Harper & Row.

Gates, B. (2006, April 7). How I work: Bill Gates. *Fortune.* Retrieved December 6, 2008, from http://money.cnn.com/2006/03/30/news/newsmakers/gates_howi work_fortune/

Goldberg, S. (2005, December). The world according to "Poor Charlie." In Kiplinger .com. Retrieved August 11, 2008, from http://www.kiplinger.com/features/archives/2005/11/munger.html

Google for Educators Discussion Group. (n.d.). Retrieved December 7, 2008, from http://groups.google.com/group/google-for-educators

Graves, D. H. (2001). *The energy to teach.* Portsmouth, NH: Heinemann.

Heat-Moon, W. L. (1999). *Blue highways: A journey into America.* Boston: Back Bay Books.

Heath, C., & Heath, D. (2007). *Made to stick: Why some ideas survive and others die.* New York: Random House.

Heath, C., & Heath, D. (2008, March). The heroic checklist: Why you should learn to love checking boxes. *Fast Company, 123,* 66–68.

Kawasaki, G. (2004). *The art of the start: The time-tested, battle-hardened guide for anyone starting anything.* New York: Portfolio.

Lynch, D. (2006). *Catching the big fish: Meditation, consciousness, and creativity.* New York: Tarcher.

Marzano, R. J. (2006). *Classroom assessment and grading that work.* Alexandria, VA: Association for Supervision and Curriculum Development.

McPhee, J. (1992). *The headmaster: Frank L. Boyden of Deerfield.* New York: Farrar, Straus and Giroux.

Morris, E. (2008, April 3). Play it again, Sam (re-enactments, part one). *The New York Times* [Electronic version]. Retrieved December 2, 2008, from http://morris.blogs.nytimes.com/2008/04/03/play-it-again-sam-re-enactments-part-one/index.html

Pink, D. H. (2005). *A whole new mind: Moving from the information age to the conceptual age.* New York: Riverhead.

Pollock, J. (2007). *Improving student learning one teacher at a time.* Alexandria, VA: Association for Supervision and Curriculum Development.

Poscente, V. (2007). *The age of speed: Learning to thrive in a more-faster-now world.* Austin, TX: Bard Press.

Richardson, R. D. (2006). *William James: In the maelstrom of American modernism.* New York: Houghton Mifflin.

Robbins, S. P. (2003). *The truth about managing people . . . And nothing but the truth.* Upper Saddle River, NJ: Prentice Hall PTR.

Schmoker, M. (1999). *Results: The Key to Continuous School Improvement* (2nd ed.). Alexandria, VA: Association for Supervision and Curriculum Development.

Scott, S. (2004). *Fierce conversations: Achieving success at work and in life, one conversation at a time.* New York: Berkley Books.

Stiggins, R. (2007). Assessment for learning: An essential foundation of productive instruction. In D. Reeves (Ed.), *Ahead of the curve: The power of assessment to transform teaching and learning* (pp. 59–76). Bloomington, IN: Solution Tree.

Stone, D., Patton, B., Heen, S., & Fisher, R. (2000). *Difficult conversations: How to discuss what matters most.* New York: Penguin.

Teacher's College Press. (2000). Thinking About Education--Approaches to Teaching [Review of the book *Approaches to teaching*, 4th ed.]. Retrieved December 7, 2008, from http://store.tcpress.com/0807744484.shtml

Vise, D., & Malseed, M. (2006). *The Google story: Inside the hottest business, media, and technology success of our time.* New York: Delta.

Index

CORWIN

A SAGE Company

The Corwin logo—a raven striding across an open book—represents the union of courage and learning. Corwin is committed to improving education for all learners by publishing books and other professional development resources for those serving the field of PreK–12 education. By providing practical, hands-on materials, Corwin continues to carry out the promise of its motto: **"Helping Educators Do Their Work Better."**